Your
HIGHEST
SELF

STRATEGIES FOR LIVING YOUR HEALTHIEST, HAPPIEST LIFE

Your HIGHEST SELF

STRATEGIES FOR LIVING YOUR HEALTHIEST, HAPPIEST LIFE

LIANNE KIM

Tanya Bay | Natalie Boese | Dr. Olivia Chu Yau | Daniela De Abreu
Julia Donnelly O'Neill | Tiomi Gao | Lynn Harrison | Jocelyn Hill
Ania Humphries | Nausheen Husain | Janice McCullough | Clare Mitchell
Andrea Mourad | Maria Munoz | Natacha Pennycooke | Kerry Rizzo
Sophie Shay | Cristina Tahoces | Dr. Stacy Thomas

TABLE OF CONTENTS

INTRODUCTION

Dear Reader,

My name is Lianne Kim. I am a business mentor, best-selling author, award-winning public speaker, and podcast host. I'm also deeply passionate about helping women live their absolute best lives possible. Let me tell you a bit about how I got here.

The concept of living life as our Highest Self has intrigued me since the very first time I heard the expression as a young woman. I have always been someone who strives to live a big life, and I've also been blessed to have a lot of ideal life circumstances. I grew up in a safe neighborhood in a developed country. I had loving parents who cared for me. I had a quality education and health care. It wasn't until I was in my twenties that I realized the life I had been living was one of privilege and not something everyone in the world has access to.

As my adult life unfolded, I found myself living in a beautiful home in East Toronto with the man of my dreams and two happy, healthy kids. We owned our own home, he had a career he enjoyed, and my business was by all accounts very successful. Life was pretty perfect.

Then, as I reached what most people would call "midlife," life started to take a toll. I was feeling sluggish and lethargic a lot of the time—that had become my new normal. I had slowly been putting on weight since having kids and didn't have the energy to do anything about it. Physically, I was no longer the fit and energetic woman I had once been, and it made me sad. Mentally, I felt foggy and not my usual sharp self.

To the outside observer, there was nothing "wrong" with me per se, but I just didn't feel like I was living life as my best self, and it irked me. After all, I didn't want to lead an ordinary life—I wanted to lead an extraordinary one. I wanted to experience great health and a clear mind. I wanted to feel joyful and abundant on a regular basis.

Instead, I found myself feeling mediocre most days, or just "okay." I wasn't sick or depressed. But I wasn't thriving either.

One day I looked at myself in the mirror. My once-toned body had lost its shape. My once-glowing, smiling face was starting to sag. My heart hurt a little looking at this woman in the mirror. *Who is she? How did she get here? And what did she do with the old me? Is this just what life looks like now? Is this just how women my age are supposed to feel?*

I decided at that moment that I didn't want to live a mediocre life, and I didn't want to feel mediocre either.

I wanted to wake up each morning feeling energized and excited to start my day.

I wanted to feel calm and centered and happy most of the time.

I wanted to feel like I had the physical and mental energy to do all the things I wanted to do in both my work and personal life.

I wanted to feel young again.

I wanted to feel inspired and excited about life once more.

I wanted to be present for my husband and kids.

I wanted to feel like I was thriving, not just surviving.

Because that is exactly what I had been doing for the past several years: just getting through the days. But it wasn't enough. I wanted more from my life and knew that in order to get that, I needed to make some changes.

So, I started making a few small changes. I started being more mindful of what and when I ate. I started making more of my own meals, using fresh ingredients. I implemented an evening yin yoga practice, which was beneficial for not only my body but my soul as well. I focused more on my breathing.

I started creating more peace in my daily life, through small but intentional practices. I started an herb garden and tended to my plants every day. I also started paying closer attention to my financial habits, which as strange as that may sound, made me feel calmer and more centered.

I began revisiting some old habits I had been neglecting. I started working out again and this time with more intention and focus. I got back to drinking two liters of water every day, a habit that had slipped away after having kids. I started journaling again. I started making time for my friendships and made a point of connecting with friends weekly.

I even started trying some brand-new things I had never done before, things that seemed almost too "out there" for someone like me. I tried cold plunging and was shocked when I liked it (up until this point, I had never been someone who enjoyed being cold). I experimented with intermittent fasting. I tried hot yoga for the first time ever, and once I got over the feeling of wanting to vomit, I was amazed and proud of what my body could do. I even played around with the idea of power posing to see if it would have an impact on my confidence levels. Sure enough, it did!

Slowly but surely, I started to feel like my old self again. But not just my "old self" . . . better!

In fact, one day I caught myself saying to a friend, "I actually feel better now than I have in my entire life," and I was in my late forties at the time.

What I didn't realize then was that I was reinventing myself, day by day, practice by practice. I was literally creating a tool kit for living life as my highest self.

But that's not even the best part.

What happened next was magical. As I started feeling better, the people in my life, namely my clients, peers, and friends, started taking notice. Many women shared with me that they, too, wanted to feel more alive and fulfilled. And that subject started coming up a LOT in my coaching work. The female entrepreneurs who I mentored all started saying things like "I know if I had more energy, I could focus more on my goals," or "I know my physical health is absolutely impacting my business results."

They knew it and I knew it: **How we feel on the inside—body, mind, and soul—is a massive determinant of our outer success.**

One day I woke up and I had done it! I felt like the woman I had always wanted to be. I felt it on the inside and the outside. And being the curious gal that I am, I wanted to understand what had actually taken place. I was reflecting on this radical transformation I had experienced. I was capturing a few thoughts in my journal about what was working well. I wanted to capture these thoughts so that if I ever started to fall off track again, I could come back to this entry and reread it, sort of like a step-by-step guide for health and success.

It was at that moment that I had an epiphany. What was working for me would likely work for other women as well! I should write a book about all of these practices so women could have access to these strategies, all in one place!

The only problem was that I knew I wasn't an expert in all of these subjects. *This will take me years to research and write on my own*, I thought. And then it hit me. The answer wasn't to write it "on my own" at all. The answer was to collaborate with other women, true experts in their fields who had done the research already. Women who had been practicing (and teaching!) these things for a lot longer than I had.

I sat down with a pen and paper and started making a list of all the women I knew who were already experts in these areas: nutrition, fitness, yoga, mindfulness, cold therapy, nature therapy, breath work, financial wellness . . . yep, I knew someone in each of these areas, and the best part was, I had already coached most of them, so I knew their businesses and skillsets intimately. I already knew the value of what they could bring to a project like this, and all I had to do was ask.

Fast-forward a few months later and we had twenty amazing female authors signed on to the project. And that project is, of course, the book you currently hold in your hands.

My wish for you, dear reader, is that you trust the wisdom in these pages. There is gold in this book! Read each chapter with an open mind (and heart). If something resonates with you, lean into it. If something doesn't feel right for you (or at least not right now), set it aside and then perhaps return to it at a later point in your journey when that concept may better serve you.

As for me, creating optimal physical, mental, and emotional health isn't a one-time deal. It's a lifelong journey. In fact, there is a good chance you'll return to this book several times over the next many months or even *years* to come. There is always more to learn and embrace, at every age and stage.

I will add that this book is not a comprehensive guide for every single success strategy available. It is meant to serve as a starting point, giving you a taste of what each of these women and their areas of expertise can offer you.

Each chapter includes a little about how the author came to find her practice, what the practice is, and why it is beneficial. Each author has also included helpful steps on how to get started implementing the practice in your own life. You will notice that some of the authors have chosen to include stories and examples from their client work. It should be noted that in these instances, some details of the experience, including people's names, have been altered to protect the individual's privacy.

I encourage you to not just read this book but to use it. Read through the tips for getting started and try some things out for yourself. And if you are seeing benefit from anything you read about, I encourage you to continue the journey. Connect with the authors, join their programs, or attend their events. Invest in further material on the areas that are working for you or even just intrigue you.

As I say, Highest Self is a journey and not merely a destination. So, please don't expect to see radical change overnight. Give yourself permission to experiment and explore, test and tweak as you go. Allow yourself the time and space to apply these tools into your life when and where it makes sense, without pressure or judgment. And most importantly, play, have fun, and delight in the process of becoming the best version of yourself.

My dear friend, I am so glad you are here.

Your highest self is waiting for you.

Let's get started!

Lianne

Chapter
ONE

SLEEP LOVE POOP

To my mom for showing me unconditional love, my dad for being my OG wellness influencer, my sister for showing me how to laugh (mostly at myself), my husband for never judging me, and my girls for raising the bar.

CRISTINA TAHOCES

Cristina Tahoces is a holistic nutritionist, TEDx speaker, and owner of Thrive Nutrition Practice. Cristina specializes in metabolic health, using bloodwork to design personalized nutritional programs, or as she likes to call them, "your own food love language." Cristina's clients optimize their metabolism, lose excess weight, and tap into the clarity, confidence, and courage they need to live their best life. Cristina is married and has two teenaged girls. She lives in Toronto but has been lucky enough to work and live in Luxembourg, London, and Hong Kong.

www.thrivenutritionpractice.com

HOW WE CHOOSE TO
NOURISH OURSELVES IS
A DAILY, INTENTIONAL
SELF-AFFIRMATION
THAT WE ARE LOVED,
WORTHY, AND
READY TO TAKE OUR
RIGHTFUL PLACE IN THE
GENERATIVE STORY OF
OUR TIME.

In 2017, a year after launching my nutrition practice, I gave a TEDx Talk called "Sleep Love Poop." During a prep session, my coach asked, "Why not call it 'Sleep Eat Poop'?" I replied, "Because nutrition isn't about eating. We all know we're supposed to eat our vegetables. The problem is that love is not the guiding force behind our eating decisions."

Sleep Love Poop is my nourishment manifesto, with love at its core. **When you eat with the purpose to sleep, love, and poop, you will come alive—just like I did, just like my clients do.**

Here are our stories:

SLEEP: THE GREAT ENABLER OF CLARITY.

Meet Katrina. The forty-nine-year-old sales executive had always prided herself on her brainpower and mental clarity. But she was losing it, and her identity, in the process. Katrina blamed it primarily on her sleep troubles. She would wake up at 3 a.m., only to toss and turn for the rest of the night. She woke up exhausted and needed copious amounts of coffee to get through the day. Her brain fog was getting in the way of her accessing the words she needed to make her pitches and arguments succinctly. All Katrina wanted was to be able to sleep more profoundly.

Katrina's nutritional assessment revealed she was snacking mindlessly on things like raisins and chocolate-covered almonds or salty pretzels and rice crackers. Her bloodwork showed high fasting glucose levels and high inflammation levels (e.g., high C-Reactive Protein). Medical researchers out of the US and Germany have proven that both high blood sugar and high C-Reactive Protein are associated with poor sleep.

We worked on nutritional interventions to lower her blood sugar levels to optimal levels, the most important one being to eat protein with every meal. This change was a challenge for Katrina who rarely had anything but coffee for breakfast and maybe paused for a quick lunchtime bagel. Nevertheless, she started having an omelet for breakfast and chicken salad for lunch. At dinnertime, she'd often opt for a quick, fifteen-minute meal of pan-fried salmon with a side of vegetables.

Adequate protein intake improves satiety and decreases sugar cravings so we can eliminate needless snacking. Within a few weeks, Katrina was able to let go of her mindless snacking habits. But the best part? Katrina's Apple watch revealed she was enjoying more time in deep sleep than before.

While Katrina's improved sleep also cleared away some of her brain fog, we did one more thing to supercharge her brain power: We increased her water intake. There are countless studies that support the connection of an old saying of mine: "Clear pee, clear mind!" Drinking more water is the most effective, not to mention cheapest, way to boost your brain power.

We should all be drinking 35 ml of water per kilogram of body weight. Unfortunately, like so many women who come through my practice, Katrina barely drank more than two glasses of water a day. She started using my favorite hack to increase her water intake: leaving a big glass of water by her bedside so that she could hydrate as soon as she woke up. Plus, she made an intentional effort to drink at least one liter of water before lunchtime.

After just one month, Katrina slept better, her brain fog had lifted, and her mental clarity had returned. She began feeling like her old self again. **Sleep and clarity go hand in hand.** But we must build sleep and clarity through the foods we eat and the water we drink. When we do that—when we eat to support our sleep and clarity—we honor our life force and reclaim the person we want to be.

LOVE: CONFIDENCE AND SELF-WORTH AREN'T FEELINGS—THEY'RE A PRACTICE.

Meet Cristina (me), a banker turned nutritionist and mother of two teenage girls. I gained fifty pounds with my first pregnancy, and they did not come off easily.

You're so fat. You're so ugly.

I hated on myself all day long. I avoided mirrors and being photographed. For years I lived a life of restriction—not just in my diet, but in life, not worthy of anything from a slice of bread to a compliment.

In addition to the negative self-talk, I was chronically sick. Every cold turned into a nasty sinus infection. I developed allergies to things that had never bothered me before, like dust. My ovulations were painful, and my skin was inflamed with hormonal acne. My body wasn't just overweight, it was falling apart, and so much so that when my maternity leave came to an end, so did my banking career.

It was a real low point in my life. I sought help and was referred to multiple specialists who treated my symptoms independently of one another. But my gut was telling me that all these seemingly unrelated symptoms were connected and rooted in deep exhaustion and depletion.

So, I went back to school to study nutrition. I figured if I could just learn the science behind how to use food to fuel my health and vitality, I could give my body a toolbox to heal.

By the time I graduated, I was thriving. I'd lost the excess weight, my skin had cleared up, my periods were pain free, and I was fighting off the viruses my kids brought home from school with ease! But it wasn't the science that had healed me. Studying nutrition helped me understand the *why* and *how* behind the rules we all grew up with, like "eat your vegetables." But there's a huge gap between knowing and doing what you should do, especially when you're constantly putting yourself down like I was.

At the beginning of my healing journey, when I looked in the mirror and didn't like what I saw, I didn't turn to broccoli to make me feel better. I turned to chocolate chip cookies, even though I was learning hard, statistical facts about how sugar would sabotage my health goals.

Eating sweet treats doesn't make any logical sense when we feel "less than," but we do it because eating isn't about logic, it's about emotion.

When we are out of love with our life and with our self, we don't turn to science, we turn to chocolate, cookies, chips, and all those sweet treats to fill our void. And yes, chips are sugar too. They are a refined carbohydrate that our body metabolizes as glucose. So, if you're thinking, *I don't have a sweet tooth, I go for the chips*, I hate to break it to you, but you do!

Our taste buds are programmed to register sweet foods as a reward because our ancestors didn't have sugar on tap like we do, and when they found a sweet patch of raspberries, they were like "Yay! We're going to live!" We are biologically programmed to eat sugar and feel safe and rewarded.

But to improve our health, we must reduce the refined sugar in our diet. That is what I did. I said, "I quit sugar!" Then one day I asked myself why I was defining success by what I was cutting out of my diet. Did it really matter if I cut out chocolate if I also wasn't having a single piece of fruit and only a tiny portion of vegetables? So, I stopped focusing on what I shouldn't eat and focused instead on reframing my food choices using the mantra "Don't give it up. TRADE UP." This mantra recruited my heart and not just my mind into making the food choices I needed to heal.

We are so used to applying this mantra to other aspects of our life: Is this the best job I can have? The best car I can drive? The best home I can live in? But we don't think of food this way. We don't think, *Is this the best way I can nourish myself given the goals I have for myself and the life I want?* No. We only use food to make ourselves smaller. **And that is the biggest mistake we women make when it comes to nutrition. We use it as a tool for restriction instead of expansion.**

Today, I eat to LOVE. I eat to show my body and mind love and gratitude for all it does for me. I learned my food love language—the foods that make my mind and body happy, the foods that help me build my immunity, lower inflammation, and support my energy levels. I practice love-led nourishment daily.

And the biggest impact? I don't need Oprah, Gwyneth, or any wellness influencer to tell me how worthy I am. I know it! Every cell in my body knows it because it hears me:

Here you are, beautiful Brain, some blueberries full of anthocyanins to fuel your memory centers. Here, my powerful Adrenals, some bell pepper to replenish your vitamin C stores so we can respond to our daily stressors but still have enough in the tank to help the girls with their math homework. Here you are, my gorgeous Gut, some fiber to help trap all those bad cholesterols and protect my loving Heart. Hello, Mama Liver, check out this yummy cauliflower, full of indole-3-carbinol to detox you from those awful estrogens that cause acne and painful periods. And my kind Kidneys, don't worry, I haven't forgotten you. Here are two liters of water to flush out heavy metals and all those toxins trying to cramp your style and life force. Not on my watch.

When self-love is the guiding force behind your food choices, you will choose life-giving food and you will feel alive. Today, at fifty years old, I feel stronger than I did in my thirties. I stand next to my girls instead of behind them to take a picture. I feel loved. I am enough.

POOP: TO LIVE COURAGEOUSLY IS TO LET GO OF THE CRAP HOLDING YOU BACK, LITERALLY.

Meet Amal, a woman who felt her excess weight was getting in the way of her social life and her career advancement. She didn't want to go out with her friends because she didn't like how she looked in her clothing. When we talked about work, she confessed she found herself talking less and less in her team meetings because she didn't want people to look at her. As a result, she felt she was going to be overlooked for the promotion she wanted. Amal was retreating into herself, and on most days, she felt utterly depressed.

Amal wanted to lose weight, but she suffered from severe constipation. Daily detoxification via bowel movements is key to weight loss. But could daily bowel movements also be key to letting go of sadness and complacency, thereby making space for more courage and motivation? I think so.

We already know that when our mental health is strong, so is our ability to step into courage. Our gut health plays a major role in our ability to support our mental health resilience via the brain–gut axis. Our understanding of the brain–gut axis is still in its infancy. However, medical research has found that constipated individuals have a 48 percent higher risk of developing depression. This higher risk could largely be attributed to the levels of serotonin that live in the gut. As we know, serotonin is our happy hormone. Low levels of serotonin in the brain can cause depression. Similarly, low levels of serotonin in the gut can cause constipation, and because information flows in both directions in the brain–gut axis, serotonin levels in the gut also affect our mood.

With these relationships in mind, we implemented the following nutritional protocols. We focused on prioritizing protein in Amal's meals. Gut serotonin levels can be influenced by eating enough protein that is rich in the amino acid L-tryptophan, which is the precursor to serotonin. Moreover, we increased her fiber intake to a minimum of 25 g every day and made sure she hit her water target so that we flushed her bowels out daily to support a healthy, flourishing gut microbiome.

When we poop daily, we clear out yesterday's garbage and keep toxins from recirculating and festering in the gut. We "Marie Kondo" our gut and thereby make room for a more vibrant, joyous community of gut bacteria.

Over the course of a few months, Amal's excess physical weight wasn't the only baggage she left behind. She let go of her fear of being seen and stepped into her courage to engage more at work and with her friends. She also learned her food love language and started to prioritize eating those foods that nourished her aliveness, in the portions that worked best for her digestive system.

Can having daily bowel movements make you braver? In Amal's words, "All I know is that it definitely feels good." Dr. Anish Sheth coined the term "poophoria" to describe this feeling of a particularly satisfying bowel movement. As it turns out, having a good poo stimulates the vagus nerve, which descends from the brain stem to the colon and causes reactions such as sudden chills and a sense of "sublime relaxation." All this time we thought courage came from "cor," the word for heart, but maybe we also have to get better at letting go of the crap holding us back.

SLEEP LOVE POOP FOR CLARITY, CONFIDENCE, AND COURAGE

Katrina reconnected with her brainiac identity and cleared her brain fog when she understood how to support sleep and clarity in her body. I reclaimed my confidence and self-worth when I started using food to love my body. Amal found the courage to rebuild her professional and personal life when she aligned her mind and body to let go of all the crap holding her back. All of us used love-led nourishment to fuel our aliveness.

HOW TO APPLY LOVE-LED NOURISHMENT:

Prioritize protein with every meal. Eat at least 0.7–1 g of protein per pound of ideal body weight to support your mental health and enable regenerative sleep.

Increase your fiber intake. Consume at least 25 g of fiber daily to support the brain–gut axis and daily detoxification. It's difficult to get to this amount without a fiber supplement. Flaxmeal has a wonderful mix of soluble and insoluble fiber that is perfect for creating bulk, trapping toxins, and creating satisfying poops.

Drink half of your body weight. Take your body weight in pounds and divide it by two—that's how many ounces of water you need to drink every single day. Hydration is the easiest way to increase your mental clarity and energy levels.

Trade up your food choices. Focus on trading up your food choices instead of restricting them. How we choose to nourish ourselves is a daily, intentional self-affirmation that we are loved, worthy, and ready to take our rightful place in the generative story of our time. Some days we might be okay to just be and simply get through the day. But on other days, we are called to perform and step into our greatness.

What do you need to step into your clarity, confidence, and courage? What can you do daily to make yourself come alive? You can eat with purpose. You can eat to sleep, love, and poop.

Chapter TWO

STRONG IS THE NEW SKINNY

To my loving husband, Sean, whose constant support and encouragement have been the rock in my journey. Your belief in me fuels my passion and inspires me every day.

ANIA HUMPHRIES

Ania Humphries brings a wealth of experience to the world of online group fitness, holding both FIS and PTS certifications. She passionately guides busy women, primarily forty and beyond, through thirty-minute efficient strength-training sessions, promoting strength, confidence, and overall well-being. Ania's commitment extends to educating women about the muscles engaged during workouts. With a personal journey of turning her own struggles into a path of wellness, she has amassed a dedicated following of clients who have found sustainable routines under her guidance. Ania lives in Toronto with her husband and two children.

www.peachyfit.ca
@peachyfit.ca_online_fitness

FITNESS ISN'T A DESTINATION, IT'S A JOURNEY OF SELF-IMPROVEMENT.

As women enter their thirties and forties and beyond, maintaining optimal health becomes increasingly important. One crucial aspect of overall well-being often overlooked is strength training, and strength training plays a pivotal role in enhancing the quality of our lives as we age. However, this way of thinking wasn't the case twenty-five years ago. Women with thin physiques were perceived as being healthy and beautiful.

If you grew up in the '80s and '90s, you were likely bombarded with the same images I was of thin women who dominated fashion magazines and television. Their often-unattainable physiques were presented as how the ideal woman should look. Unfortunately, these unrealistic images influenced an entire generation of women to jump on the treadmill and burn calories.

In 1997, I purchased my first gym membership. The "women's" section was in the basement of the facility and had no natural light. It had some weight machines, a rack of dumbbells, and numerous treadmills filling more than half the room. In comparison, the main co-ed weight room was beside big bright windows in a prominent spot on the main floor, but there were never any women there. It was a room full of men with huge muscles. It wasn't a welcoming experience, and I found it quite intimidating. Plus, I'd have no idea what to do even if I did step in there.

I have been passionate about fitness for most of my life. The gym was my safe place where I could sweat, let go, de-stress, and focus on myself. I would plug in my music, run, and use the time to think. But after getting married and having kids, my fitness regimen took a backseat. I had two amazing children and a job, and every moment of my life was spent taking care of other people. I felt busier than ever and fell into a routine where others were always my priority. I found myself carrying an extra twenty to thirty pounds, and I had a weak posture. I'd hardly look at myself in the mirror, and when I did, I did not like who I saw. My confidence took a hit, my anxiety surged, and I didn't have the energy for anything. The inner voice in my mind was narrating everything in my life negatively. I had fallen down a rabbit hole of insecurities.

I gave myself many reasons for why I looked and felt the way I did: motherhood, my job, and the lack of time in the day to do anything else. But the reality was, my kids were seven and eight, and they weren't stuck to my hip. I needed to evaluate what was really holding me back. Was I busy? Yes. Was I tired? Absolutely. Was I stressed? Definitely! As I asked myself these questions, I realized they weren't valid reasons—they were just plain old excuses fueled by hesitation over putting in the work and a fear of failure.

There was a moment one night as I was going through my routine of getting ready for bed when I paused to give myself a really deep look. It felt as though I could see right through myself, and the truth was staring back. At that moment, I mentally told myself, *Enough! No more.* The next morning, upon waking, I challenged myself to make it my mission to confront my inner voice and start making changes in my life that were going to make me feel proud and good about myself.

Recognizing I needed a change, I decided to prioritize my health again and return to working out and being mindful of my diet. I knew it wasn't going to be easy. I had to break an eight-year habit by disrupting the routine and lifestyle I was accustomed to. I knew I would be taking a journey down a different path and incorporating some new lifestyle changes. And despite the challenges of finding the time to do so with two kids and a job, I committed to treating my workouts as nonnegotiable appointments in my calendar.

I started carving out time with brief sessions three days per week. I incorporated the elliptical and Stairmaster machines for ten to fifteen minutes and gradually made my way up to thirty to forty minutes, sometimes using the weight machines for variety and fun. My extra weight was slowly coming off, but not as rapidly as it had in my earlier years. Despite my consistent exercise routine and cleaner eating, I found my energy levels still remained low, and I felt burned out. In general, I was looking skinnier, but my overall image in the mirror didn't look healthy.

As I started going to the gym consistently, I noticed a fellow parent from my kids' school who worked out at the same time as I did. She was about my age and height, and we had similar builds, yet she radiated strength and vitality. Her posture was amazing, she stood tall, and she had the nice-looking shoulders I'd always longed for when I put on a pretty dress to go out. We'd smile and say hello to one another in the locker room, but when I went to the cardio area, she would primarily hit the weights.

I was six months into my new gym routine when I finally made the connection that our different workouts were yielding different results. It was like the world opened up before me. It was a revelation! This was where I needed to be! I saw what was possible, and it wasn't from spending hours on the treadmill. It was about embracing strength and incorporating lifting weights. I left the gym that day after making an appointment with a personal trainer. I started shifting my mindset and began a new journey with goals that included lifting heavy things. I knew it wouldn't be a walk in the park or a slow jog on an inclined treadmill. This was a journey where sweat and discomfort were going to be a part of my life, and I could not have been more excited about it.

A month into training with my trainer, COVID-19 brought everything to a halt. I was navigating online school with my kids, and my husband worked remotely from our home. It was a major adjustment, to say the least. My fitness routine stopped, my stress levels soared, and I found comfort in alcohol. As the months passed, the consequences became clear: weight gain, escalating stress, disrupted sleep, and an overwhelming feeling of suffocation within the walls of my own home with the people I loved most dearly. It didn't take me long to realize that this wasn't a sustainable or healthy path for me. I again committed myself to living differently. I thought, *I'm better than this. I deserve more. I wouldn't treat a friend like I'm treating myself.*

WHY STRENGTH TRAIN?

One of the realizations I made on this new journey and recommitment to being my best self was my desire to help people. I decided to pursue my personal trainer and fitness instructor specialist certifications. By helping other people become stronger and healthier, I could also help myself. I also wanted to set a good example for my kids. I started working out at home, and I loved it. Once I started lifting weights, I was standing taller, my mind was clearer, I was sleeping much better, I had more energy, and I felt stronger; when I looked at myself in the mirror, I saw a side of me I hadn't seen in a long time—I was feeling and looking healthy. So, I took the leap and started my own online group fitness and personal trainer business, PeachyFit. I wanted to encourage busy women that they, too, could find time in their day to feel good and be the best versions of themselves by lifting weights.

The most frequent misconception I hear from clients and friends is the fear of gaining too much muscle and becoming too bulky. **The fact is, muscle mass decreases by approximately 3–8 percent per decade after the age of thirty, and this rate of decline is even higher after the age of sixty.** Many of my clients express their desire for a toned appearance without developing the muscles of a bodybuilder. But becoming bulky takes years of dedication, and it requires a certain type of training. Becoming bulky doesn't accidentally happen.

Strength training is not just for bodybuilders or athletes, and it's not meant for just men. Strength training is essential for everyone, and it has numerous benefits as we age. But according to the US National Center of Health Statistics, only 26.9 percent of women are participating in strength training.

So why should we be lifting weights after forty and normalizing it into our routine like brushing our teeth?

Mental health: Strength training reduces stress, boosts confidence, increases sleep quality, and improves mood. The release of endorphins during exercise can create a feeling of happiness and contribute to a more positive outlook. It offers a holistic approach to better equip us with the ups and downs of life. Sweat today so you can thrive tomorrow!

Increased metabolism: As we age, there is a natural slowdown in our metabolism. However, when we engage in strength training, our metabolism boosts. When we build muscles, we are effectively increasing our resting metabolic rate, which simply means that when we are sitting on the couch or sleeping, our body is burning more calories than it would if we had less muscle mass, making it easier for us to manage our weight.

Bone health: Strength training is a powerful tool for our bones. After the age of thirty, our bones reach a mineral peak in bone density followed by a natural decrease, making them more susceptible to fractures. Strength training strengthens our bones and joints and may reduce the risk of osteoporosis.

Independence as we age: Strength training can help carry our day-to-day activities with greater ease, whether it's unloading groceries, climbing stairs, enhancing athleticism, or simply having more energy to play with our kids and grandkids. Strength training improves posture and balance, ultimately helping us maintain our independence as we age.

Most people understand the importance of regular exercise for their physical, mental, and emotional well-being. However, maybe you've never felt fit and think it can't happen for you. Maybe you feel you're too old or too tired or too busy to try something new. Maybe the thought of doing something by yourself and for yourself is scary. Would it help you to know that even half an hour a day would benefit you?

Both the World Health Organization and the Centers for Disease Control and Prevention recommend at least 150 to 300 minutes of moderate exercise or 75 to 150 minutes of vigorous aerobic exercise a week for adults up to age 64, and to do strength-training exercises for all major muscle groups at least twice per week. This equals about 30 minutes a day, which is doable for most.

HOW TO FIND YOUR STRENGTH:

Having an accountability partner to support you can increase your chances of sticking to your routine. It can be a friend, a family member, or even a coworker who has similar fitness goals and can encourage and motivate you. Each morning before I begin my class, my husband prepares a cup of coffee for me and fills my water bottle. In return, I help him by organizing his workouts and ensuring he follows through and shows up. Small gestures like these can have a significant impact on your fitness journey.

You may not always feel motivated. When I'm lacking motivation, I find Mel Robbins's five-second rule helps—you need to move your body before your brain figures out what you're doing. I count down from five, and once I get to one, I start moving.

Fitness isn't a destination, it's a journey of self-improvement. For anyone embarking on a fitness journey, the initial step should involve creating a well-defined plan. **Just as we set S.M.A.R.T. goals in our professional lives, the same principle applies to our fitness journey.**

Specific: Clearly outline what you want to achieve. Instead of saying, "I want to start lifting weights," be specific. For example, "I want to strength train two days a week for thirty minutes for the next three months."

Measurable: Determine how you will track your progress. Add the dates you would like to work out into your calendar and treat them as nonnegotiable appointments.

Attainable: Set realistic goals that you can reach, especially if you are just starting. Diving into an hour-long workout four days a week is not going to be sustainable. Work on showing up for yourself first rather than on the intensity of the workout. Building habits comes first.

Relevant: Ensure your fitness goals align with your life. If you're a hockey mom and you need to be at the arena on Saturday mornings, avoid this time to work out, even if you think you can just "squeeze it in."

Time: Set a specific timeframe to reach your first fitness goal. For example, if you've committed to working out twice a week for two months and you successfully achieve this milestone, celebrate this win and consider other ways to further enhance your plan and goals. It's important to gradually build a solid foundation and achieve smaller goals before fully committing in order to avoid burning out prematurely.

Working out with a personal trainer (like me!) can help you achieve your goals. A trainer can build a plan that is suitable for you, educate you in how to prevent injuries, be your cheerleader, and keep you accountable. I'm here to make sure you're living the best years of your life. Life will only get harder if you don't make the change today. And if not today, then when? When are you going to stop making excuses and start prioritizing yourself? Don't wait for the perfect time to commit because focusing on "perfect" will only hold you back. Getting healthy and building strength is a lifestyle, not a seasonal hobby.

Live your life around making yourself healthy and happy by being kind to yourself instead of fixating on your imperfections.

When I was younger, I worked out because I was inundated by unattainable images of thin women. But now that I'm educated on what I need to be healthy, I work out because I want to be strong, because I want to promote body positivity for my children, and because I want to enhance the quality of my life so I can feel good and stand tall and confident. Today, I work out so I can help others understand that strong is beautiful and **strong is the new skinny**.

Chapter
THREE

RECHARGE & THRIVE: THE TRANSFORMATIONAL POWER OF SLEEP

To my family: I will forever be grateful for the lessons you teach me, your unfaltering support, and the joy you bring to my life!

JANICE MCCULLOUGH

Janice McCullough, an occupational therapist, is passionate about helping others not only improve their sleep but also achieve personal fulfillment by tapping into their inherent wisdom and strengths. Throughout her nearly twenty-year career, Janice has supported individuals of all ages and abilities on their journey toward mental health and well-being. Her entrepreneurial experience began with a focus on sleep when she became a mother to two rambunctious boys. Since then, it has expanded to include coaching services designed to help people build meaningful, engaging, and purposeful lives. She feels honored to walk alongside her clients and bear witness to their resilience and brilliance. Janice resides in St. Albert, Alberta. When she's not aiding others in their quest to thrive, she enjoys spending time with her family—particularly in nature—or reading while cuddling with her large lapdog.

www.restisbest.ca

@wellness_through_sleep

THE LINK BETWEEN
SLEEP AND SUCCESS
IS UNDENIABLE,
FORMING THE CRITICAL
FOUNDATION FOR HOW
WE SHOW UP EACH DAY.

I see you. You've got a lot going on, a plate heaping with responsibilities. It is so easy to exchange sleep in favor of completing your to-do list or indulging in more entertaining activities. Sleep is often simply more expendable than all the other priorities in your life.

I see you managing it all, but you feel stressed, tired, and drained. You may be forgetful, have trouble staying in the moment, or find it difficult focusing on things even when they interest you. You're irritable, impatient, and anxious. You feel isolated.

I see you lying awake when you'd like to be asleep, your mind racing and occupied with self-criticisms, anxiety, or thoughts about tomorrow. You may spend time worrying about not being able to sleep. And when you do *finally* fall asleep, you are woken up by a full bladder, a child, your partner, or a noise. Whatever the cause, you are awake now and feeling frustrated.

I see you because this was me. I understand.

As a young adult, I had always been able to fall asleep as soon as my head hit my pillow. I had fewer responsibilities and took sleep for granted. When my first child was born, this changed. I remember thinking my son was the worst sleeper in the world! I wasn't sleeping because he wasn't sleeping. When, *miraculously*, he did sleep, I prioritized cleaning the house, working on my education and job commitments, and completing anything else I thought needed doing. But I became unhappy and discontented with my constant state of overwhelm. Fortunately for me, a simple change had a significant positive impact on my life, and it can for you too.

What if I told you that simply prioritizing sleep can help decrease overwhelm, improve your mood, health, and cognitive functions, and increase your work and life satisfaction? Would you believe that sleeping more is the key?

Right before my second child was born, I took a professional development course focused on sleep health. While I sat in the lecture hall, a lightbulb went off. I needed more sleep! Why hadn't this clicked during the hundreds of times I had supported my clients in finding strategies to help them feel more rested? I felt foolish that it had taken me so long to connect the dots. I decided to focus on getting more sleep. The impact it had on me both personally and professionally was staggering. Since then, it has been my honor to share my passion for the transformational power of sleep with hundreds of people, in various stages of life, and to learn about the positive changes it has brought to them.

Interestingly, despite these abundant testimonials about the life-enhancing benefits of sleep, I often find myself reverting to old habits. Why does this happen when I know how essential sleep is? Well, it is almost always due to my misplaced focus on achieving specific goals such as a cleaner home, getting more work done, or increasing the time spent performing more visible forms of self-care. Why do these tasks gain my focus to the detriment of my sleep?

Our beliefs and values impact our sleep, and this mindset is shaped by our environment. Society values missed sleep. Statements about staying up all night are often made with a mix of exhaustion and pride in the voice of the teller. Lost sleep is somehow an indicator of the commenter's dedication to a task or the amount of fun they had. However, these lost hours of slumber often result in outcomes contrary to our intended objective. In her book *The Sleep Revolution*, Arianna Huffington explains, "We sacrifice sleep in the name of productivity, but ironically our loss of sleep, despite the extra hours we spend at work, adds up to 11 days of lost productivity per year per worker."

Phrases such as "I can sleep when I'm dead" prioritize all other activities above rest. This unconscious undervaluing, coupled with our daily grind, portrays slumber as secondary to our quest for productivity. The value that we place on tangible results leads us to devalue seemingly unproductive tasks. And while most would say that sleep is important, would we also describe it as productive?

In his book *Why We Sleep: Unlocking the Power of Sleep and Dreams*, sleep expert Matthew Walker states, "There does not seem to be one major organ within the body, or process within the brain, that isn't optimally enhanced by sleep." If this is the case, sleep seems pretty productive to me. In fact, research has shown that it is critical to overall performance and well-being. A lack of sleep has a direct, negative impact on a person's body, mind, and spirit, which also affects emotions, temperament, and self-control.

The link between sleep and success is undeniable, forming the critical foundation for how we show up each day. Adequate, quality time in slumber is intricately tied to our health, well-being, and relationships. Sleep is not just another pillar of our health, it is the bedrock the pillars are built upon. Sleep deprivation impacts cognitive functions, including memory, learning, attention, and concentration. A lack of focus can reduce our engagement with other people, hindering effective communication and our ability to connect with them.

When we are fatigued, we tend to be more reward-seeking and impulsive. Are you trying to break a habit? Spending more time asleep could help decrease the reward-driven decisions that perpetuate the unwanted behavior.

A well-rested mind is more resilient and adaptable, enabling individuals to navigate challenges with clarity and creativity. Those executive functioning skills required for goal-directed behavior are enchanced with adequate sleep. How could more clarity, creativity, and increased focus on your goals improve your day-to-day life?

Sleep is essential for emotional regulation and self-control. Irritability and decreased empathy, as well as feelings of isolation, depression, and anxiety, are common for people who spend less time asleep. When you're tired, heightened emotions can lead to more intense feelings of overwhelm, stress, and anger, and reduce your ability to cope with these emotions. If you struggle with anxiety and depression, or other mental health concerns, you may have a harder time getting enough quality sleep, which will exacerbate your mental health symptoms.

When we are weary, we are less likely to engage in a healthy lifestyle, but this exhaustion impacts our physical health at a much deeper level. Sleep is crucial to overall health, supporting immune function, aiding in recovery from daily stressors, and allowing the body to repair and rejuvenate. Poor sleep has been connected to insulin resistance, glucose dysfunction, and increased feelings of hunger. **Simply put, a lack of sleep can lead to a wide range of health problems, including Alzheimer's disease, obesity, heart disease, high blood pressure, diabetes, and stroke.**

Some of the world's greatest catastrophes are thought to be, at least in part, due to insufficient rest, including the Chernobyl nuclear disaster (1986), the Exxon Valdez spill (1989), the American Airlines flight 1420 crash (1999), etc. You might not operate a nuclear reactor, sail an oil tanker, or fly an airplane, but your decisions may still impact the health and well-being of others. When tired, we are often unaware of our cognitive dysfunction. For example, microsleeps are brief, involuntary episodes of sleep that last up to thirty seconds and can occur when a person is fatigued and performing a monotonous task. During microsleep, parts of the brain fall asleep while others remain awake, resulting in impaired attention and performance. If this happens while you are driving, it can have fatal consequences. According to the Sleep Foundation, in the US, drowsiness is a factor in approximately 21 percent of fatal crashes, which is nearly as high as the 30 percent of fatal collisions due to intoxication.

These impairments may seem far-fetched, but when you regularly get fewer than seven hours of sleep per night, you begin to experience this detrimental decline in your health, well-being, and ability to show up and thrive. Investing in sleep will unlock your full potential, thus creating a longer, more fulfilling, and accomplished life.

HOW TO INVEST IN SLEEP:

Fall in love with sleep. Walker confesses to being "in love" with sleep and states that he gives himself a nonnegotiable eight hours of time in bed every night. Let's be honest; there is no way you will be able to consistently allocate a third of your day (seven to nine hours) to doing something you don't love! If you feel rest is something that comes second or stands in the way of other aspects of your life, you will not be able to prioritize it long-term.

This requires a mindset shift: changing your thoughts, beliefs, and attitudes. How can sleep become something you look forward to? My clients and I discuss how their lives might look different should they get more sleep. What do you hope to gain from getting more restorative rest? Take time to consider what this means for you; visualize the transformative impact sleep will have on your life.

Create an oasis. When I began working on improving my sleep, I transformed my bedroom. I hadn't invested effort designing my room like I had with the more public spaces of my home. During this bedroom makeover, I invested in blackout blinds and decor I found calming. I found sheets I loved (cooling sheets because I run hot) and installed a ceiling fan. I removed excess electronics and minimized clutter to increase tranquility. I added a plant because I'm most relaxed when I'm near nature. I focused on creating a space that aligned with my new goal to love and prioritize rest and rejuvenation. Does your bedroom promote the feelings of peace and tranquility necessary to promote sleep? If not, what do you need to do to change that?

Maintain a schedule. I feel best when I have eight to eight and a half hours of sleep, so I give myself a minimum of eight and a half nonnegotiable hours in bed each night. Most days I need to be awake at 6 a.m., which means I need to be in bed with my lights off by 9:30 p.m. It can be difficult to keep this bedtime. The evening can fly by, and before I know it, it is almost midnight. To rectify this, I set an alarm for 9 p.m., allowing time for my bedtime routine.

Our body's clock thrives on consistency, and some of us are more sensitive to changes than others. If you struggle to fall or remain asleep, a regular wake time can be just as important as bedtime. Your sleep drive gradually builds during the day, creating pressure to help you fall asleep at night. When you spend extra time in bed, you limit the opportunity to build this pressure. I often find it difficult to fall asleep at night after sleeping in on the weekend, which means less night sleep and a cranky, coffee-focused mama the next day! Since I am sensitive to inconsistent wake times, I try to keep my morning routine the same every day. Maintaining consistent wake and bedtimes optimizes your internal circadian rhythm and allows the opportunity to build your sleep pressure.

Does this mean you have to have a perfect, consistent schedule? No. Obviously, as with all things, you need to have some flexibility, but if you find that you are struggling to sleep despite giving yourself ample time in bed, you may want to see how you can create some more consistency.

Can't sleep? Get up! When you are struggling to fall asleep and remain in bed, you condition yourself to pair your bed with whatever it is keeping you awake. For example, if you lie in bed worrying for extended lengths of time, your brain learns that bedtime equals "worry time." This unintentional pairing increases the likelihood that it will happen again and again. The next time you are struggling to fall asleep, be it at the beginning, middle, or end of the night, get up and do something else. When you feel sleepy again, return to bed. Repeat as necessary.

When you are tired, it can be hard to think of things to do while you wait to feel sleepy. Pre-emptively creating a list of activities (e.g., reading, crafting, journaling, stretching, or visualization) can help. Using electronics is not recommended, but if you want to use a screen, be mindful to block out blue light by using a filter on your device or blue-blocking glasses. Screen time, exercise, and housework may hinder you from being able to get back into a sleepy state and should, for most people, be done with caution.

Take daily pauses. Stress can accumulate during your day, and just like a kettle releasing steam on the stove, a mindful pause to breathe or move your body provides the opportunity to release the pressure. By intentionally planning stress-reducing activities into your day, you can prevent this buildup and make it easier to achieve restful slumber. Discover what helps you to decompress, then engage in it often throughout the day!

Live a sleep-promoting lifestyle. Consider the lifestyle components that may be hindering your ability to sleep. These factors may include:

- Not getting adequate hydration: dehydration hinders regulation of body temperature, which can disrupt your night.
- Consuming caffeine, alcohol, and nicotine close to bedtime: these substances can cause difficulties falling asleep or interfere with your sleep's architecture.
- Not eating a well-rounded diet: make sure to get plenty of vitamin B, C, D, and E as well as magnesium and iron.
- Remaining inactive: ensure that you move your body daily.

Consider sleep context. Many clients initially seek me out for support with their own sleep, but my involvement sometimes expands to support others in their home. Sleep is impacted by routines, habits, beliefs, and lifestyle that are often shared by families. It makes sense that people in the same house may share difficulties achieving restorative slumber. A family member may be the main cause of your own sleep concerns. A partner's snoring may keep you awake (regular snoring should always be investigated as it can decrease sleep quality, leading to serious health implications such as stroke). Your child may take hours to fall asleep at night, leading to working late into the night to make up for "lost time." In both cases, addressing these contextual factors will positively impact your own sleep.

Remember, sleep is not a luxury but a necessity, providing the essential foundation that enables you to succeed. If you have tried to improve your sleep but are still struggling to feel rested, speak to a physician to rule out underlying medical conditions. If you struggle to fall or stay asleep or wake before your desired wake time, three or more times per week for three months or more, it may be time to consult a professional trained in cognitive behavioral therapy for insomnia. In this case, reaching out to a professional, like me, can be life changing.

Prioritizing sleep can be daunting: achieving restorative rest may seem counterproductive to fulfilling daily commitments, engaging meaningfully with others, and pursuing leisure or wellness pursuits. Perhaps because we are not awake to witness the transformational power of sleep, it can be easily dismissed and undervalued. Regardless, the truth remains unchanged: sufficient, quality sleep is at the core of our health, well-being, and resiliency. It enables us to show up as our best self. We truly can transform with better sleep, so give yourself permission to sleep, recharge, and thrive.

Rest well!

Chapter FOUR

THE FAR-REACHING
BENEFITS OF FLEXIBILITY

To me at ages seventeen, thirty-two, and thirty-eight, for trusting my body to lead me through the challenges of womanhood, and to all the women who stay by my side every step of the way. And to my boys and my husband for encouraging, supporting, and cheering me on, even through my wildest adventures.

DANIELA DE ABREU

Daniela De Abreu is passionate about community and bringing people together through her work, something she's accomplishing day by day with BeForYou, her yoga studio. In it she has created a space for women to unite through movement and meditation, both of which have helped her connect with others as well as deeper to herself. She loves to travel, host friends at her home, and create new ways of connecting with friends and family for an enjoyable time. She is married with two young boys.

@bforyou_yogawellness

EMBRACE THE POWER
OF STRETCHING AND
FLEXIBILITY, FOR THEY
ARE THE KEYS TO
UNLOCKING YOUR FULL
POTENTIAL.

Growing up, I longed to be a dancer, but I was painfully aware that I didn't have a "dancer's body." I didn't fit the mold instilled in me that one needed to dance, so I didn't pursue it. And so it was with yoga. When I first thought about yoga and imagined the person practicing it, I envisioned someone long, lean, graceful, and naturally flexible. Basically, someone the opposite of me.

Unfortunately, it's common for some living in Western society to think that in order to practice yoga, you must fit into what society has dubbed as the "yoga body." What we seem to have forgotten, or haven't learned, is that yoga is meant for everybody. Literally, every BODY can do yoga, and you don't need to be a contortionist to practice! **In fact, you don't need flexibility to practice yoga. You gain flexibility by doing yoga.** And I'm not only referring to the ability to stretch for your toes.

I first began my yoga journey on a whim. I was eighteen, working the desk at a chiropractic clinic. I'd help out occasionally with the patients when one of the practitioners needed a hand, and I enjoyed the interaction. The chiropractor, noticing my interest, encouraged me to take some training courses so I could get more involved with the patients and help them with their rehabilitation, and I thought taking a course to help with their stretches would be beneficial. Then, one day on my way home from work, I saw a notice for yoga training, so I walked in and asked about it.

"You're interested in training? Great. How long have you been practicing yoga?" the woman at the front asked me.

"Oh, I've never actually tried it," I responded nonchalantly.

I was young and naive, but I agreed to sign up for one class before I decided whether to commit. During that first class, I experienced a roller coaster of emotions: frustration over what I couldn't do, pride in what I could do, curiosity about the way my body reacted, and a sense of calm I hadn't felt before. I was hooked! Yoga seemed magical to me, so I enrolled in the training program on the spot.

As I delved deeper into my yoga journey, I discovered the importance of stretching and functional movement. I also learned how to take the modality of yoga and translate it to our daily activities to ensure we avoid injuries while doing the most mundane of them. I loved being able to share my knowledge with the patients at the clinic. From there, I moved on to teaching yoga at the studio where I received my training. As I expanded my practice and increased my flexibility, an interesting thing happened: I felt I was being stretched in more ways than just physically. I was gaining confidence and becoming more emotionally resilient. I felt more open and flexible with what life brought me.

I moved cities, then provinces, but the one constant through life's changes was yoga. It never wavered, and it helped me find friends and work wherever I went. I always had a community because of yoga, regardless of what was going on in my life. Now, don't get me wrong, my practice was nowhere near perfect, and throughout the years it's changed quite a bit. But what has not changed is the dedication I have to use yoga the best way that suits me. The flexibility of the practice has helped me during each life milestone.

SOMETIMES, THE GREATEST WAY TO HEAL IS TO MOVE.

I had my first child when I was thirty-two, by way of cesarean section. I was overjoyed at becoming a mom, but I was in pain from the surgery and couldn't get back to my regular movement for months. When I finally healed, I began feeling extreme soreness in and around my lower back—it was my body telling me I needed to get back to yoga. This awareness came with age and my practice. My teenaged self never would have understood that the soreness would be eased by moving my body and rehabilitating the injuries rather than simply resting. I began slowly. I gave myself twenty minutes a few days a week to move, and I used simple postures and stretches, just enough to reintroduce my new body back to the practice.

Moving my body postpartum looked very different than it had before. I found myself in a similar position a lot of newcomers do when trying a class for the first time. I was uncoordinated, uncomfortable, and unaware of this new body I was living in. I had been here before—this uncertainty, lack of body awareness, discomfort. But it was this experience of reintroducing myself back to a practice that my body needed in order to feel functional. I felt new to yoga and my body, but I had the trust that this practice was available to me no matter where I was on my journey. It was during this time I had the initial spark to open a studio for women. I wanted to remove the stigma surrounding yoga and allow this practice to be accessible for women at all stages and phases of their lives.

I remember talking in the park with other new moms on mat leave. Several of them mentioned they wanted to look a certain way *before* they joined a gym or yoga studio. There was so much focus on how they looked on the *outside*, but none on the way they felt on the *inside*. Because they felt they didn't "look the part," they weren't taking the steps needed to recover from injuries or move their body to help prevent future injuries. They weren't joining classes where movement and meditation could help in every aspect of their lives.

My dream was to open a studio where women would feel accepted for who they are and where they are in their fitness journey. Yoga taught me that I'm strong and flexible and that there isn't one ideal body type required for practicing, which is something I felt passionate about sharing. After the birth of my second son, I realized that dream by opening BeForYou, a women's yoga studio. I leaned on flexibility in my approach by tailoring our program to each teacher's area of comfort. By offering various types of yoga, each teacher has been able to tap into the message they want to share with the clients, which is a beautiful thing.

Stretching and movement provide so many benefits to our overall health, particularly as we age. According to Dr. Howard E. LeWine of Harvard Health Publishing, "Stretching keeps the muscles flexible and healthy, and we need that flexibility to maintain a range of motion in the joints. Without it, the muscles shorten and become tight. Then, when you call on the muscles for activity, they are unable to extend all the way. That puts you at risk for joint pain, strains, and muscle damage."

Flexibility extends beyond just the physical realm; it plays a significant role in our mental and emotional well-being as well. I had bouts of postpartum depression after the birth of both my sons, but I know that the emotional foundation I have from yoga helped me immensely. I used meditation and breathing to center myself and heal, and I accessed tools learned in the practice to reduce my stress, increase my energy, and boost my confidence.

Flexibility also helps with balance, which goes hand in hand with injury prevention. Imagine a world where you can confidently navigate through life without worrying about falls, sprained ankles, or pulled muscles. The muscles you build and stretch help improve your range of motion and keep those accidents at bay. Stretching also promotes proper posture. Not only will you stand taller and appear more youthful, but you'll also feel stronger and more confident.

Engaging in flexibility exercises increases blood flow to your muscles, boosting oxygen and nutrient supply, which helps you minimize the mid-afternoon slumps. So, whether you're chasing after your kids, grand-kids, or pets, good flexibility ensures you'll stay upright and smiling.

HOW TO INCORPORATE FLEXIBILITY INTO YOUR LIFE:

Start by setting aside just a few minutes each day to dedicate to your flexibility practice. YouTube tutorials can be incredibly helpful resources to guide you along the way. You can incorporate simple stretches into your morning routine, or perhaps relax at night with a short yoga session. Find a comfortable space in your home, roll out a trusty yoga mat or blanket, and let your body guide you into gentle movements. Embrace the opportunity to reconnect with your breath, allowing it to guide you deeper into each stretch. Remember, simplicity is your ally as you embark on this journey. Start with basic standing poses, such as Mountain Pose or Forward Fold, gradually exploring deeper stretches as your confidence grows.

Incorporate stretching breaks throughout your day. Set a timer on your phone or computer to remind yourself to take short stretching breaks. This can help counteract the stiffness and tightness that can come from sitting for long periods. Aim to hold each stretch for twenty to thirty seconds to see improvements in flexibility over time. If you're consistent, you will definitely see results!

Attend a beginner-friendly yoga class. Many yoga studios offer classes specifically geared toward beginners or those looking to improve their flexibility. These classes typically focus on gentle stretching and breathing exercises that can help increase flexibility.

Join a dance or movement class. Dance classes, like ballet or modern dance, can be a fun and creative way to improve flexibility. These classes often incorporate dynamic stretching movements that can help increase flexibility in a more engaging way. Plus, you'll get to learn new skills and enjoy the social aspect of dancing with others. You'll lift your spirits and use your muscles.

Be conscious of choosing to move. Simple everyday actions such as walking, bending down to pick something up, and taking the stairs all engage your muscles. Try to incorporate as many as you can into your daily routine. You'll be surprised at the cumulative effects!

Flexibility is not just physical—it's a tool to transform your mind, body, and spirit. You are stronger than you know, and through movement, you have the power to achieve anything you set your mind to. So, keep stretching, keep moving, and never underestimate the incredible impact it can have on your life. Embrace the power of stretching and flexibility, for they are the keys to unlocking your full potential. Reach for them with open arms and a flexible heart.

Chapter FIVE

THE MIRACLE OF MEDITATING

To my children, who taught me the true meaning of mindfulness and gave me the courage to embrace self-compassion and meditation.

DR. OLIVIA CHU YAU

Dr. Olivia Chu Yau is a licensed clinical neuropsychologist working with pediatric and adult populations in Ontario. She created the Centre for Neuropsychology and Emotional Wellness with a team of mental health providers to provide psychodiagnostic assessments and treatment to children, adolescents, and adults. The goal of the center is to rewire brain connections to help people achieve mental and emotional wellness. Olivia is passionate about finding ways to help people who struggle with emotional and cognitive difficulties. In her spare time, she enjoys listening to podcasts or audiobooks, being active outdoors, and trying different cuisines. She lives in Toronto with her children.

www.cnew.ca

@cnew_clinic

MEDITATION LEADS
TO CELL GROWTH
IN THE BRAIN THAT
HELPS US LEARN NEW
THINGS, CONTROL
OUR EMOTIONS,
AND UNDERSTAND
OURSELVES.

@cnew_clinic

My first introduction to meditation was in my twenties at the end of a yoga class. We were asked to lie down on our mat in silence in savasana. I remember thinking it was a waste of time because I was there to improve my physical flexibility, balance, and strength. The act of just lying down seemed counterproductive. My savasana time was me thinking about what I needed to do after class or for the week until the instructor told us it was over.

In graduate school, a couple of my classmates suggested taking some deep breaths to help calm the mind. I tried doing it a few times when I felt nervous, such as before a presentation or a test. Although it seemed to calm the nerves in that moment of breathing, all the anxious thoughts came right back as soon as I started the task. I also remember one of my classmates sharing that she enjoyed participating in a day of silent meditation at a retreat. I was bewildered by how being silent all day alone would be fun or enlightening. I saw myself as a doer, and meditation seemed to be doing nothing.

WHY MEDITATE?

As I started my career as a psychologist, I began learning about the impressive amount of scientific evidence behind the practice of meditation. It has been found to lower systolic and diastolic blood pressure, improve sleep quality, and decrease the sensation of pain. When people learned how to meditate, brain imaging showed the areas related to self-regulation of pain were activated. Meditation also significantly decreases the objective and subjective symptoms of anxiety and depression as well as feelings of stress. Research showed these changes continued to last long-term (six months to two years) after the meditation program finished.

Additionally, researchers at Harvard Medical School found that meditation can lead to changes in brain gray matter concentration. Individuals who participated in a Mindfulness-Based Stress Reduction program that involved mindfulness meditation for eight weeks had their brain scanned with an anatomical MRI before and after the program. The MRI found that those who did the meditation compared to individuals who had not done the meditation had changes in gray matter concentration in brain regions involved in learning and memory processes, emotion regulation, self-referential processing, and perspective taking.

Mindfulness practice leads to increases in regional brain gray matter density; this means that meditation leads to cell growth in the brain that helps us learn new things, control our emotions, and understand ourselves. **That's the miracle of meditating. What I thought was merely doing nothing was literally making brain cells grow!**

I knew my clients wanted improvement in many of the areas meditation had proven to help. So, I took a course with Jon Kabat-Zinn that opened my eyes to the immense power of this practice. I also read remarkable books on the topic, including *Wherever You Go, There You Are: Mindfulness Meditation in Everyday Life* by Jon Kabat-Zinn, *The Miracle of Mindfulness* by Thích Nhat Hanh, and *The Power of Now* by Eckhart Tolle. When I started doing guided meditation practices with my clients, I saw how their visibly anxious demeanor changed to become calmer and more grounded. I witnessed how some of my clients who had suffered from chronic pain for years no longer experienced pain while engaging in meditation. I noticed how after meditating, they were better able to get in touch with their innermost emotions and vulnerable thoughts, which helped us accomplish more in our therapy sessions. My clients who meditated outside of our session got noticeably better at understanding themselves and others around them. They reported feeling less stressed and better able to manage their negative emotions. Imagine our capacity to manage stress as a meter, and our meter goes up as we encounter stressful situations. Doing meditation regularly is like resetting the meter so we are better able to handle life stressors.

Although I had read the impressive science behind it and witnessed all the changes it was making for my clients, my mind created many reasons why I shouldn't meditate: I was too busy. Making time for meditation seemed difficult when I was trying to balance work, family, and social life. I seemed to be doing okay without it. Did I really need it? It didn't seem to fit my personality. I was someone who liked to think and analyze. I probably wouldn't do it right. It was hard for me to clear my mind and be still.

But if I was really being honest with myself, the biggest reason why I didn't want to do it was because I was scared to be alone with my thoughts. What if I found out I had dark thoughts? What if I found out something about myself I didn't like? What if meditation changed who I was for the worse? It was the fear of the unknown coupled with self-criticism. Once I got over this through self-reflection and self-compassion, I allowed myself the opportunity to give meditation a real try.

> **It's important to remember that there is no way you can do meditation incorrectly as long as you are trying to focus on the awareness of the present moment.**

There is no shutting off your brain. In my first meditation class, I tried so hard to stop my mind from its incessant chatter. I was surprised by how often I judged everything, including my own ability to meditate. I was critical of myself for drifting off into my thought cycles. But as I got deeper into understanding meditation, I learned that the mind's continuous thinking is a part of meditating. The mind will want to plan, judge, worry, problem solve, and generate stories or narratives because our mind is pretty darn good at doing that and is used to doing it fairly automatically. **The intention of meditation is not to clear your mind but to bring awareness into the present moment.** Some days I am able to have moments of silence in my brain. Some days my brain cannot stop thinking of things. Most days my meditation looks like this:

Okay. Breathe. Breathe in and out.
Breathe in.
Breathe out.
Follow the breath.
In.
Out.
Oh, I forgot to respond to the email from Richard. I better get on
that and do it right after I am done. And I have to register for

Susanna's summer dance camp by tomorrow before it gets full. I should write it down later.

Wait, I'm meditating. Right. Back to breathing.

Breathe in and breathe out.

In.

Out.

This feels good. I feel calm. Relaxed. Not like how I felt yesterday when I got all frustrated at Lincoln. I know it was because I was feeling tired at the end of the day and wanted him to sleep so I could get my own time. I should try to go to sleep earlier and get more rest. I know it makes me feel better. Tonight, I will try to go to bed at a decent hour. Get off the computer by 10 p.m. Oh, I'm supposed to be meditating. I got lost in thought again. Let's focus back on the breath.

In.

Out.

Most of the time it's a mix of my mind wandering and my mind focusing solely on the breath. But I've stuck with it and have begun to see results. I've started having more energy and motivation. Before meditating regularly, I was usually mentally and physically fatigued after going to work, taking care of the kids, and doing household chores. I longed to just mindlessly watch television or scroll social media while snacking on popcorn at night. But after meditation, I feel less fatigued by the end of the day. There are more days I am able to do work or read after I put the kids to bed. It becomes easier to follow my exercise routine rather than putting it off. It's like giving your mind a break from all the continuous thoughts you have. When you allow yourself to pause, you actually have more energy to engage in tasks you need to get done.

Our minds are constantly running; think of meditation as you taking a break from jogging by sitting on the bench for a little while to give you the energy to keep going.

I'm now able to better focus, get more accomplished, and feel less distracted by my internal thoughts. As a mom and business owner, I have a never-ending list of things I need to get done. I used to feel scattered. Sometimes I would start something and then midway through the task, I'd remember I had to do something else. So, I would go do that task and then forget about the task I was doing before it. After meditation, I can stay more focused on my current task, and as a result, I get more things accomplished. Research shows meditation improves your ability to sustain your attention and increase creativity. I am able to make new connections to things in my work and personal life I did not realize before, and I've some aha moments that are unforgettable.

I've gotten better acquainted with myself. **In the process of trying to clear my mind and focus on breathing, I've created space for me to observe my own thoughts without any usual distractions.** I am finally able to see my own train of thought. I see what types of thoughts pop up in my mind and how I react to them. In the same breath (pun intended), I have become more aware of the complexity of feelings during meditation. I've realized how I used to react to a single thought with panic or fear because I took it as though it were the truth, then I often felt ashamed or disappointed in myself. I've now started watching my thoughts and feelings with a sense of curiosity. I've discovered that some of my frequent thoughts and feelings are not serving me well because they are contradictory to the type of person I strive to be. When they come up again in my daily life and meditation, I let them go by reflecting on how they are not useful to me. Instead, the thoughts and images that bring me joy, peace, and love I repeat with gratitude and appreciation.

Instead of having a knee-jerk reaction to thoughts or feelings, I make conscious choices in my response. These changes have led to me making better decisions and engaging in actions that are more in line with my life goals.

I feel calmer and more grateful for life. There is an inner sense of serenity, like everything is all right in the world and I will be okay. When stressful things happen, I am less likely to get frustrated, or if I do get frustrated, I don't stay irritated for as long as I used to. There is a feeling of safety in life that even if something unexpected or unwanted happens, it really isn't the end of the world. It is this experiential sense of knowing things will be okay rather than knowing it logically. Most days I feel life is pretty great—I wake up and go to sleep grateful to be alive and living my life just as it is.

Once you feel the changes from meditation, you'll want to keep doing it. It's addictive. I always feel better after meditating, even when I have a day when my mind doesn't stop thinking. Some mornings I set an intention for my day during my meditation, and it helps me try to keep that intention for the day. There have been times when I didn't meditate for a few days, and I noticed a difference in myself; I seemed more irritable, more distractible, and less able to be present in the moment. Alternatively, I've had moments during and after my meditation when I feel pure bliss. It is like those moments when you feel as if time has stopped and everything is just perfect. I think all of us would love to have more of those moments in our life.

HOW TO BEGIN MEDITATING:

When I first started meditating, I used a guided meditation where someone talks you through focusing on different sensations in your body along with your breath. There are different apps and videos you can find to help you start meditating. Although this helped me get comfortable with meditation, the real change for me started after I did a meditation group course that taught me how to do self-guided meditation daily. It is completely different when you have to consciously lead your mind to non-thinking rather than actively listening to someone instruct you to non-thinking.

Schedule it. Like any new habit, you need to intentionally make time for it by putting it into your daily schedule. When I first started, I set time in the morning after I dropped off the kids and before I started my work schedule, as well as during my lunchtime. I began with brief sessions to set myself up for success. I set my alarm for three minutes of meditation each day, then gradually increased the time each week until I got to thirty minutes of meditation.

Find your space. Find a quiet spot where you feel safe and won't get distracted. Sit up in a comfortable place with your eyes closed.

Just breathe. Notice your breathing. Focus on the breath coming in and the breath leaving the body. Without trying to change the breath in any way, just notice it. Follow the cycle of breath moving in and out of your body.

Your mind will start to wander from the breathing. You will get caught up in the thinking and get carried away. At some point you will realize you should focus on the breath. Do not get disappointed or critical if you get distracted and are not able to focus on the breath. Rather, try to focus your attention back on the breath again.

Keep at it until the alarm goes off. (On some days it will feel as if time stopped, and you will be surprised when the alarm goes off because it felt as if you had just started meditating. On other days it feels like you've been meditating forever.)

Open your eyes and continue on with your day while experiencing the benefits of meditation.

If you are still asking yourself if you need meditation, the answer is a resounding yes. If you are someone who wants to thrive in your life, then you need meditation. It is a lot like getting proper sleep. Sure, I can survive on five hours of sleep, but I cannot thrive on five hours of sleep. The beauty of meditation is how simple and natural it is because all you have to do is focus on something you are already doing every second: breathing.

Chapter SIX

REDEFINING SELF-CARE AND SELF-LOVE

To my children, Marcus and Maya. You are my dream come true.

ANDREA MOURAD

Andrea Mourad is a best-selling author, a former elementary school teacher of fifteen years, the co-owner of two award-winning Korean skincare companies, Saranghae and Orora Skin Science, and a mentor to female entrepreneurs. It was through her road to entrepreneurship that Andrea realized the only way to achieve true success in life was through prioritizing her self-care and total well-being. She is now on a mission to empower other women to start behaving as the main character in their lives and to then elevate their self-care rituals by focusing on small daily habits that have the absolute power to transform them. Andrea lives in Toronto with her husband and their two abundantly joyful children. They spend most of their time hiking, biking, exercising, dancing, traveling, cooking, and gardening together.

www.lovesaranghae.com
@ororaskin

JUST AS A BEAUTIFULLY
NOURISHED PLANT
BLOSSOMS WITH
LASTING, VIBRANT
BLOOMS, OUR
ABILITY TO RADIATE
POSITIVITY AND LOVE
WHILE CONTRIBUTING
POWERFULLY TO
THE WORLD HINGES
ON THE INTENTIONAL
NOURISHMENT OF OUR
OWN MIND, BODY, AND
SOUL.

For many of us, in the pursuit of giving joyfully to others, we often overlook the fundamental truth that self-care is not a luxury but an essential, foundational part of our overall well-being. Just as a beautifully nourished plant blossoms with lasting, vibrant blooms, our ability to radiate positivity and love while contributing powerfully to the world hinges on the intentional nourishment of our own mind, body, and soul. Embarking on a journey of self-care is, at its core, an act of self-love. In a world that often glorifies relentless hustle and grind, we must recognize that nourishing ourselves is not a frivolous indulgence but instead a testament to the love and respect we show to ourselves each day. From the invigorating rhythm of a morning run to the gentle touch of an evening skincare routine, all can represent an expression of affection toward you, the self, that carries you unconditionally through life on this beautiful planet.

When I was growing up, I didn't have many examples of strong, powerful women who took good care of themselves. The women in my life, most of whom are of Middle Eastern and European descent, worked hard, whether it was inside the home or out. They were strong in the sense they managed an incredible load, caring for their families as well as tending to their demanding careers. However, regardless of the type of work they did or the number of mouths they fed, they all shared one thing in common . . . a sadness or sense of unfulfillment inside of them that, no matter how hard they tried, could not be masked. They didn't often speak of their pain, but it was felt. You could see it in the ways they showed up for us as children, for their spouses, and for the world around them. There was never a question of whether we were loved, but we unquestionably carried their struggle and unfulfillment, in our own unique ways, all throughout our lives.

When I ask myself what was missing from the souls of these beautiful women who raised me, the following comes to mind: that spark of joy in their eyes, a childlike playfulness and laughter, a sense of hope for the future they dreamed of having, and simply an inner sense of peace that naturally comes with leading a satisfying, fulfilling life. Ultimately, in my humble view, they were missing their self-care rituals, which at their core, translate to self-love.

I never witnessed any of the women in my life sitting quietly reading a book or attending an art class. I never saw them going for a morning run or taking a nightly bath. I never saw them doing a skincare routine or a meditation, and I certainly never saw them sitting down to eat before anyone else, even if they were tired or hungry. These were my first examples of what being a woman was like.

Years later I carried that vision into the teaching career I chose, then into my own family. I continued to make choices and allow habits to be created that facilitated this notion that women are supposed to struggle and be givers in spite of themselves. I also gave my husband and my son everything from the depths of my soul. If I'm being completely honest, sometimes it felt genuine, but most other times it felt forced. I was constantly pouring from an empty cup, and after a while, it didn't feel good. Regardless of how I felt, however, this was the story I had created in my mind for what a woman was, and I found a great deal of comfort in this familiarity. I believed, like the women before me, that these were the sacrifices I needed to make in order to have what I considered to be a happy home. There was only one very big problem with all of this: I wasn't happy.

As Rumi said, "Never give from the depths of your well, but from your overflow."

After the devastating miscarriage of my baby girl Elia, and another miscarriage shortly after, I knew something big had to change. I knew inside that this wasn't how my story was supposed to go. I needed to rewrite this story of mine to include me as the main character in my life and not a supporting one. I began paying more attention to the nudges inside my heart and started caring more about what I wanted. It was then that I made a promise to myself to start listening to the whispers within. I would reject all judgments about what came up for me, and I would instead simply observe. I began to reflect on meaningful questions to discover my innate truth: *Who am I without all these roles to perform? Do I like what I've become? If not, why not? What would I love instead? What brings me joy and peace? What makes me feel truly alive?*

This mindset shift opened a whole new world for me. I started getting creative. Ideas flowed. I practiced saying no and setting boundaries, despite how others felt about it. I took responsibility for everything that my life was and began creating the life I truly wanted. There was no more living on the sidelines in default mode. I began by carving out just ten minutes a day to do something just for me that lit me up. I first committed to working out. Then I added a morning and evening skincare routine. Next, I added journaling and quiet reading time. From there, it continued into a comprehensive daily self-care practice that continues to evolve as I do. What began as a nudge of curiosity inside my heart turned into tiny stepping stones toward a happier, healthier, more expansive me.

Through working in the skincare and wellness industry for some time now and speaking to thousands of women from all cultures, religions, and socioeconomic levels, it has become clear to me that there are so many others out there, especially mothers, who are struggling to carve out time in their days to do things that light them up. Many don't even know what lights them up anymore, or worse, they feel an incredible sense of guilt for even entertaining the thought. As a result, these women have shared that they are exhausted, resentful, overstimulated, and completely unfulfilled. So many mothers have told me that they've lost themselves during motherhood and don't know who they are anymore. We must ask ourselves why. Why does this happen to so many women after having a baby? Why do we allow it?

We need to change the narrative around what a woman is and should be after motherhood and then reevaluate how we behave and what we allow going forward. We need to start paying attention to what we need and want, even if it means the demands on our loved ones become greater.

When we introduce ourselves in various contexts, we often say our names and include some variation of our titles. Those labels define and categorize us in the world in which we live. I am a mother and a wife. I am a teacher, a skincare and wellness entrepreneur, and a mentor. I am an author (and so many other titles). Most importantly, though, I am me—a human experience that exists among billions of others yet is completely unique, as there is no one else anywhere in this world with my exact fingerprint. Why then do we choose to act from a place of our titles and groupings instead of our individuality? Why then, after motherhood, do we often forget that although we are so much to so many, we are first our own unique person?

When you hear the term *self-care*, what comes to mind for you? How does that word make you feel? Do you feel a judgment associated with the term? Do you feel that self-care isn't available to you for one reason or another? Or do you see self-care as an act of self-love and regularly prioritize it into your daily life? Wherever you are at this moment is entirely okay. The most important part here is that you are honest with yourself about where you are. From this place of vulnerability, we can all surely grow.

WHAT IS SELF-CARE?

Self-care to me refers to the intentional actions and practices that individuals undertake to prioritize their physical, mental, and emotional well-being. It is an act of self-love to make time for oneself, and it involves activities and habits that promote health, reduce stress, and enhance overall quality of life. Self-care can take various forms and is highly personal as it involves identifying and engaging in activities that bring a sense of fulfillment and rejuvenation to the individual.

Since self-care is such a broad term, I break it down into categories of care: physical well-being (e.g., exercise and proper nutrition), mental and emotional well-being (e.g., meditation and journaling), social connections (e.g., spending time with loved ones), boundaries (e.g., learning to say no and time management), hobbies and leisure pursuits (that bring joy and a sense of accomplishment), personal development (that pushes us to grow outside of our comfort zone), and rest and relaxation (how we recharge our batteries and promote healing). I break this general self-care term down into categories mainly so one can see that self-care can be many things and doesn't have to involve an expensive spa day to be effective. You also don't need to do all of it all of the time. What I do suggest, however, is that you plan to engage in at least some of these activities within the various categories every day. Rest and relaxation, for example, should be built into your daily routine. Going to bed at a reasonable time and protecting your evening routine to ensure consistent, quality sleep is a daily practice that will surely benefit your overall health and well-being.

We often downplay the significance of skin-to-skin contact when thinking of how we can take better care of ourselves. It encompasses self-nurturing but is something we don't always associate with self-care. Introducing self-care routines that involve touch, like skincare routines or facial massages, can profoundly influence our mental and physical well-being. These instances of self-connection and self-care provide an opportunity to slow down, stay in the present moment, and foster a deeper sense of self-love and acceptance. In a world often dominated by screens and virtual communication, we must not underestimate the importance of genuine human contact. Among the many benefits of self-care as a whole, through physical touch we release oxytocin, strengthen connections, alleviate stress, and support emotional regulation. Whether shared with loved ones or practiced on ourselves, these moments of nurturing contact play a crucial role in promoting mental health, healing from trauma, and enhancing resilience.

HOW TO IMPLEMENT A SELF-CARE ROUTINE:

Make a daily plan. Set boundaries around this sacred time and do not negotiate it, with yourself or anyone else. Put it in your family calendar for all to see.

Change it up. During this scheduled time, engage in different activities for variety. For mental and emotional well-being, for example, perhaps you might engage in a meditation. For physical well-being, perhaps you might go for a brisk walk in nature. On another day, you may instead choose to take a nap. All are perfect.

If you aren't sure which of these activities will be enjoyable to you, make a list of things you think you might love to do during your special time and try something from that list each day.

Pay attention. In the beginning, monitor how you feel going into the activity, during it, and afterward. Do more of what lights you up and continue to observe. How do you approach tasks that you engage in after your self-care time? How do you show up with those you love? These observations will be your guide for how you will continue to take better care of yourself.

Let go of the worry. There is no right or wrong way to do self-care. The most important thing to remember here is that you are making a commitment to love yourself more every single day because you are the most important person in your life. I know that's hard to hear, especially for us mamas, but it is the honest truth. No one in your family will be okay if you are struggling.

Remember, as the women before me set an example of what womanhood was to them, you are undoubtedly setting an example for your children as well. Instead of showing them that it is a hard role and one that requires you give in spite of yourself, show them that prioritizing yourself is a healthy and essential part of your well-being. Demonstrate that it is okay to take time out to rest and do the things you love, even if you are a busy parent and have a growing career. By loving yourself the most, you are giving your children permission to love themselves the most too. This, to me, is one of the most powerful gifts you can ever give to your children simply by committing to loving yourself first every day.

Self-care is crucial for maintaining overall well-being and preventing burnout. **Self-care plays a vital role in contributing to a happy home, promoting resilience, reducing stress, and enhancing one's ability to cope with life's challenges.** I strongly believe that it is the best way to lead a fulfilling, meaningful, and successful life. The specific self-care practices can vary from person to person based on individual preferences, needs, and lifestyles, so just be consistent and engage in activities that truly make you feel rejuvenated and alive. Ultimately, you are the leading role in your life, and it's time to start acting like it. You are worthy. You are enough. You are so very loved.

Chapter SEVEN

STAND UP FOR YOUR HEALTH

To Darren and Maya: You have taught me that movement really is medicine.

JOCELYN HILL

Jocelyn Hill is a board-certified integrative health coach and founder of J Wellness. She coaches high-performing women who want to take charge of their health and aging. Jocelyn believes we are in control of our health destiny by the choices we make every day. By engaging her clients in the practices of lifestyle medicine, she uses proven tools and methods to help them prevent, treat, and even reverse disease. Using a highly customized and integrative approach, she helps her clients make sustainable changes so they can start flourishing. Jocelyn lives in Toronto with her husband, daughter, and dog.

www.jwellness.ca
@_jocelynhill

YOU CAN HARNESS THE POWER OF THE MIND-BODY CONNECTION SO THAT YOU'RE GETTING THE MOST BENEFIT FROM EVERY MINUTE YOU'RE MOVING.

@_jocelynhill

We are in the midst of an epidemic of chronic disease related to our modern lifestyles. Our level of activity has greatly diminished due to modern inventions and technology. We attend Zoom calls, binge our favorite Netflix shows, and sit and scroll social media. According to the World Health Organization, sedentary behavior now ranks among the ten leading causes of death and disability in the world. It is estimated that 60–85 percent of people in the world—from both developed and developing countries—lead sedentary lifestyles.

Even if you're a fairly regular exerciser, you might be surprised to find out that you may qualify as sedentary. A sedentary lifestyle is one that involves sitting for most of the day. This generally means someone who spends six or more hours per day sitting or lying down (screen time, driving, working, reading), and they lack significant movement in their daily lives.

I'm a national board-certified health and wellness coach, and even my lifestyle became a bit stagnant a few years ago. I had never thought of myself as being "sedentary." Yet when I took a good hard look at my lifestyle in 2017, it became shockingly apparent that I wasn't moving enough for optimal health and well-being. A good wearable such as an

Oura ring will show you precisely how many hours you've been inactive. On a typical day, I drove my daughter to school, then I went to the clinic where I sat with patients for most of the day (9–5 p.m.). After work, I drove home and sat down after dinner to catch up on emails and social media. I remember having busy weekends with activities and family, and there wasn't always enough time for exercise.

As a full-time health coach, I was busy supporting other women with their health goals and habits. I saw firsthand how difficult it was to prioritize clean eating, getting enough sleep, and exercising regularly. My biggest challenge had always been with exercise. I knew all about the benefits of movement, but I wasn't doing enough about it on a consistent basis. And I just knew it was time to level up my own movement game.

Dr. Robert Butler, former director of the National Institute on Aging, said, "If exercise could be packed in a pill, it would be the single most widely prescribed and beneficial medicine in the nation."

This quote completely reframed exercise for me. I've also been influenced by Dr. John Ratey, Harvard psychiatrist and author of *Spark: The Revolutionary New Science of Exercise and the Brain*. Ratey called physical activity, "A little bit of Prozac, and a little bit of Ritalin" and "Miracle-Gro" for the brain.

There are five main ways I've increased and diversified my own movement and helped my clients do the same.

1. Change your overall mindset about exercise.
2. Just sit less every day.
3. Add in more N.E.A.T. (accidental exercise).
4. Find what moves you and do it.
5. Be intentional and really commit.

How you think about your daily movement is probably affecting your health and well-being more than you know. Even when you don't make it to the gym or do your favorite class, you can still benefit from incorporating movement into your day. You can also harness the power of the mind–body connection so you're getting the most benefit from every minute you're moving.

Harvard psychologist Ellen Langer has published several important studies about the effects of perception on physiology. One provocative study looked at whether our perception of how much exercise we are getting has any effect on how our bodies actually look. To do this, she studied hotel maids. While the work of chambermaids is physically strenuous, the participants didn't see it as exercise. In fact, they didn't see themselves as physically active because "exercise" happens "before or after work." Interestingly, more than one-third of participants reported they didn't get any exercise at all.

Study participants were randomly divided into two groups: one group wasn't given any information at all. The experimental group, however, was taught that their work was exercise, just like specific exercises found at a typical gym. The only difference between the two groups of eighty-four maids is that one-half believed their work was exercise. As a result of the change in mindset, the experimental group showed significant changes: their body mass index declined, they lost weight, their blood pressure came down, and their waist-to-hip ratio decreased.

According to Dr. Langer, "Mind–body unity means that everything we do, experience or think is relevant to our health." One implication of the aforementioned study is the importance of mindset in cultivating a healthy active identity. Reflect on all the ways you're moving your body as you go through your day and take a moment to appreciate your body and reflect on the benefits. Even on days when I'm not doing "formal" exercise, I always think of myself as a very active person because I know it's having an impact on my health, well-being, and longevity.

THE PROBLEM WITH SITTING:

It might be surprising to learn that many people currently spend more time sitting than sleeping. The key is to find a balance between sitting, standing, and generally moving around.

It has been said that chairs are junk food for the body. Sitting has also been referred to as "the new smoking." Sitting = stagnation, which is a toxin no different from any other (such as harmful fats). When you sit you use less energy than you do when you move or stand.

Too much sitting contributes to depression, anxiety, obesity, diabetes, high blood pressure, unhealthy cholesterol, weak bones, and many other chronic conditions. On top of that, we slouch, tense our shoulders, and stay in unnatural positions for long periods, which contribute to low energy and many aches and pains.

The good news for all of us is that it's easy to offset the damage of sitting and mitigate the ill effects. The solution is simple: When you sit less and move more, you will look, feel, and function better.

HOW TO INCORPORATE MOVEMENT INTO YOUR DAY:

Stand a minimum of once an hour. Moving from sitting to standing can significantly increase your energy consumption. You can try setting an alarm on your phone to build the habit.

Stand if you plan to scroll social media. I promise you won't spend as much time on it as you would if you're sitting.

Stand up when you take or place a call. It's a great way to break up an hour of sitting.

Increase your daily movement with N.E.A.T. exercise. The most underappreciated activity is what you do as you move about your day—from playing with your kids to doing the dishes to strolling with your dog. Another way to think of this movement is "accidental exercise."

N.E.A.T. stands for non-exercise activity thermogenesis and is the energy used and the calories burned from everything outside of eating, sleeping, and regular exercise (for example, running or resistance training). N.E.A.T. exercise is important because it can amount for a significant portion of your daily energy expenditure. Think of it as movement breaks throughout your day to stretch your muscles, clear your mind, and help you stave off weight gain. When you boost your N.E.A.T. daily, you can also boost your fitness and your mental health.

A major benefit is that despite minimal perceived effort, they burn anywhere between 300–1,000+ calories a day. What I used to think of as annoying chores, such as loading the dishwasher, are now opportunities to boost my N.E.A.T. And I am actually a N.E.A.T. fanatic. I just didn't know it, and I certainly wasn't aware of the many benefits until a few years ago.

I've become very conscious of my N.E.A.T. activities, and I build them into my day. This is beneficial on days when I don't have time for formal exercise. I focus on staying in motion throughout the day and reflect on how active I've been to take advantage of the mind–body connection from the study. Pay extra attention to N.E.A.T. exercise to cultivate a more active identity.

Some of my favorite ways to boost N.E.A.T. include stretching upon waking instead of reaching for my phone—this increases flexibility, improves circulation, and relieves tension. I also use music when I'm doing chores. Music can enhance the intensity and enjoyment of virtually any activity. Additionally, I store frequently used essentials in a low cupboard or drawer. You'll end up squatting down and standing up several times a day.

When you feel active, you are much more likely to continue making healthy active choices.

Find what really moves you and do it. After changing my mindset, sitting less, and boosting my N.E.A.T. exercise, the next shift I committed to was walking more. I knew from my training and experience that if you don't find an activity you enjoy, you are less likely to do it when you need it the most—when you're stressed out and pressed for time.

I've experimented with virtually every type of workout and class in the past twenty years, and nothing has had more of an impact on my overall health and well-being than walking.

I love virtually every type of walk—from strolling with my dog, to mindful walks in nature, to vigorous hikes. Walking has also been my go-to favorite exercise at every age and stage—from being a sleep-deprived new mom to a dog mom to an empty nester.

As an integrative health coach, I'm well aware of the many impressive and powerful health benefits of walking. It grows brain cells, lifts our moods, unleashes our creative juices, fires our muscles, and so much more. Top scientists and experts all agree on how walking can change our health, and our life. For example, according to Dr. Sara Gottfried, "A walk a day keeps breast cancer away."

Neuroscientist Shane O'Mara, author of *In Praise of Walking: The New Science of How We Walk and Why It's Good for Us*, says walking is holistic: every aspect of it aids every aspect of one's being. O'Mara says, "It's interesting to think of walking as a self-administered pill produced in our own bodies."

It's relatively easy to incorporate extra steps into your day. I start every day with a morning walk. This is a win-win because getting ten minutes of daylight before 10 a.m. also does wonders for your circadian rhythm and sleep. I swear by a quick walk at lunchtime or in the after-noon between meetings. It only takes a few minutes to get a completely different perspective or to simply boost your energy. Additionally, I walk my dog for ten to fifteen minutes every night after dinner. This tends to be a slower-paced walk, but it's still long enough to supply many health benefits such as balancing blood sugar levels.

I love recommending walking to people. It is one of the easiest and most beneficial ways to build activity into your life. It can be done socially, or alone, and best of all, it can be squeezed into the busiest of lives. I always encourage people to look for small opportunities to squeeze in a few extra steps everywhere they go. If you've been a bit sedentary but want to begin a new routine, ten to fifteen minutes of walking is a good starting point. I find myself saying to friends, family, and clients, "Go for a walk and everything will feel better."

Be intentional and really commit to being more active.

Like many of my clients, I used to have a love–hate relationship with exercise. I knew it was good for me, and I really enjoyed it, but even so, I didn't always do it. Despite all my good intentions, life often got in the way. I found it really easy to put off exercising until "tomorrow."

Part of my problem—or should I say my "challenge"—was finding the time in my schedule for exercise as well as committing myself emotionally to doing it. I removed the pressure of having to get in a class or workout and started enjoying moving my body. Very often when people say they don't have time to walk or move or work out, what they really mean is they haven't made it a priority.

When I became more intentional about increasing my daily movement, I started to see gains in virtually every area of my life.

Stand up for your health. No one else can do it for you.

Research shows that just working small, extra movements into your day has amazing health benefits. Back in 2017, I started shifting how I moved, when and where I moved, and even how I thought about my daily movement. As a result of incorporating these strategies, I can honestly say I feel stronger and more energized in my fifties than I did in my thirties.

I've worked with so many women who were like me a few years ago. They simply don't realize they are living a stagnant lifestyle. Even when they do formal exercise, many women are sedentary for the rest of the day.

The good news is that you don't have to hit the gym several times a week, you just need to prioritize exercise. Whatever it is, no matter how big or small, just move more. And I always encourage people to focus first on the mental and emotional gains after they move their body, instead of focusing on the physical benefits, which can take much longer to become obvious.

Start moving more today, and you'll positively affect your health in the short-term (better energy, focus, and mood), medium-term (improved sleep and hormone balance), and long-term (prevention of many chronic conditions and diseases).

Chapter EIGHT

UNLEASH YOUR VOICE TO DISCOVER YOUR POWER AND PURPOSE

To Aunty Dean, who continues to teach me ways to stand in my power decades after her death. To my younger eighteen-year-old self: moments were taken away, but you continued on. I am proud to have given you the grieving and healing you were seeking and deserve. To my husband, thank you for always holding space for me, for being my lifelong best friend, and for loving me unconditionally. To my son, always remember the power you hold. You are my greatest story.

NATACHA PENNYCOOKE

Natacha Pennycooke is an award-winning psychotherapist, international speaker, The Accelerated Leader™ mindset and leadership coach, a corporate consultant, and the visionary CEO of Natacha Pennycooke Psychotherapy (NPP) group practice. Renowned for her work in guiding high-achieving professionals toward mental and emotional well-being, Natacha's core belief is that understanding the power of the mind is crucial to unlocking our greatest potential. She expertly guides individuals to shift their mindset from internalized limiting beliefs, impostor syndrome, self-doubt, and fears toward empowerment and purpose. Natacha's approach not only fosters personal growth and mental resilience but also inspires individuals to create the thriving lives they aspire to live. Residing in the greater Toronto area with her high school sweetheart–turned husband and their son, Natacha enjoys spending quiet time in nature near flowing water and indulging in her love for popcorn.

www.natachapennycooke.com

@natachapennycooke.therapy

YOUR VOICE, YOUR
STORY, AND YOUR
TRUTH ARE THE LEGACY
YOU LEAVE BEHIND—A
TESTAMENT TO YOUR
COURAGE AND A
BEACON FOR OTHERS.

From an early age I knew my voice had power. I have always been a passionate person whose energy is felt when I enter a room. At eighteen years old, I lost my voice when my aunt died. To be clear, I could speak, but I lost parts of the passion and energy that had encompassed a vital part of me. My aunt was a beautiful soul who was vibrant and loud; she commanded attention, spoke up, and did not let obstacles stand in her way. She was the age I am now (as I write this chapter) when she died. My cousin, her daughter, says I look exactly like her. Losing my aunt changed the trajectory of my life.

For decades I felt I was not allowed to grieve her death. Sounds foolish, right? I thought it was a privilege that wasn't accessible to me because I hadn't attended her funeral. On that day, I'd had an exam. My parents, struck with their own grief, void of supportive emotional regulation skills, and coming from a culture whose expectations are "education first," did not know it was acceptable to miss an exam due to a family death. So, I went to my physics exam and cried the whole time. Needless to say, I failed—and I was not permitted to do a rewrite or to repeat the class. My only option for continuing my post-secondary education was to choose a new field of study. I was devastated I would not reach my dream of being a marine biologist. Instead, I decided on my plan B: to pursue a degree in psychology.

In many ways, psychology saved my life. Learning about human behavior, cognitive thoughts, mental health disorders, and the vastness of our emotions not only gave me an outlet for my many pent-up emotions, but it also provided me with vital context for my family dynamics and the impact on my inner self. Connecting the importance of our feelings, understanding how life events set our foundation, and learning theories of behavior completely shifted my perspectives on the world around me. This new level of awareness reinvigorated a passion as I became more aware of my inner self and what she needed to heal so I could thrive in this world.

The state of my inner self (like for many of you) had experienced changes throughout my life due to various life and traumatic events. Unfortunately, these events have left unseen scars; however, they have also left a lifetime of learning, resiliency, and tools that are now a part of my ever-growing toolbox. It's a toolbox I have unlimited access to in order to support myself, the hundreds of people I have helped, and the countless numbers of people I will help in the future.

One of the most essential tools I use is on the self and self-talk. More specifically, it's on how we speak with and to ourselves, how we can affirm ourselves using positive affirmations, how we gain power in sharing our story, and how talk therapy can help unpack blocks and lead us to find our voice and live in our joy.

WHAT IS SELF-TALK?

As a psychotherapist, one of the most common questions I get asked is: "Is it normal to talk to myself?"

Talking to oneself is a fairly normal and common experience for all people. Talking to yourself, or self-talk, is defined as the ways in which one speaks to themselves; it is your internal dialogue, inner narrative, or inner voice, which can be either an inner critic or inner motivator. Despite the notion that "only smart people talk to themselves," people of varying education levels, cultures, and social-economic statuses use self-talk. Self-talk can be categorized as either positive or negative.

Negative self-talk refers to an internal dialogue or thoughts that individuals have about themselves that are predominantly critical, doubtful, or self-defeating. It involves the habit of using negative language and focusing on one's perceived shortcomings, failures, or limitations. **Negative self-talk creates an unhealthy inner narrative and has a detrimental impact on one's emotions, self-worth, and self-esteem; it can have a harmful outcome to overall psychological and physical well-being.**

Examples of negative self-talk include thoughts such as:

I'm not good enough.

I always mess things up.

I'll never succeed.

Have you said words like these to yourself?

This type of self-talk can contribute to feelings of inadequacy, increased self-doubt, anxiety, and low self-esteem. It may also hinder personal growth and achievement by creating a self-fulfilling prophecy where individuals start to believe and act in ways that align with these negative thoughts.

Recognizing and challenging negative self-talk is an important step in promoting a more positive and constructive mindset. Talk therapy can help individuals recognize, challenge, and change negative thought patterns to improve their internal dialogue and adopt a more positive self-talk behavior, thus improving mental well-being.

Important note: Contact your primary care provider and/or a licensed mental health professional if you are experiencing any of the following:

- *loud or erratic self-talk or muttering accompanied with heightened levels of fear, worry, stress, or sadness*
- *hearing other voices in your head talking to you*
- *a decreased ability to function in your daily life, a cognitive disturbance, or potentially harmful self-talk due to a traumatic event*

Positive self-talk refers to the practice of using optimistic and supportive internal dialogue or thoughts to encourage oneself, boost confidence, and cultivate a positive mindset. It involves consciously replacing negative, unhealthy, or self-defeating thoughts with healthy constructive messages and affirming statements. **Positive self-talk can contribute to improved self-esteem and motivation; it can have a significant impact on our mental well-being, our self-worth, and our overall mindset.**

Examples of positive self-talk include thoughts such as:

I am capable and resilient.

Every challenge is an opportunity for growth.

I celebrate my achievements.

Have you said words like these to yourself?

By adopting a positive internal narrative, you can enhance your ability to cope with stress, setbacks, and difficult situations. This optimistic mindset and thought pattern can also contribute to increased resilience and a more positive outlook on life.

Developing positive self-talk often involves self-awareness and intentional efforts to challenge and reframe negative thoughts. Positive self-talk and the use of positive affirmations is a key component of my therapeutic practice where we utilize approaches like culturally adaptive–cognitive behavioral therapy, narrative therapy, emotional regulation, and

Afrocentric strength-based practices, all of which aim to help individuals challenge and change their thought patterns and develop healthier ways of thinking.

SO, HOW DO YOU CHANGE NEGATIVE SELF-TALK TO POSITIVE SELF-TALK?

Use the 3 C's of self-talk: Catch, Challenge, Change

Catch: This involves catching or becoming aware of your thoughts and recognizing when negative or unhelpful self-talk occurs. It is about catching those thoughts in the moment as they arise.

Challenge: Once you have caught your negative self-talk, the next step is to challenge those thoughts. Question their validity and consider whether they are based on actual evidence or are a product of distorted thinking and false reality. Challenging these negative thoughts with more positivity and a realistic perspective will help change them.

Change: After challenging negative self-talk, the goal is to change those thoughts into more constructive and positive ones. Replace self-defeating thoughts with positive affirmations or more realistic and positive statements that promote healthier thoughts and a positive mindset.

HOW CAN YOU EMBRACE POSITIVE SELF-TALK?

As previously highlighted, engaging in positive self-talk is a vital and beneficial habit that plays a crucial role in shaping our mindset and contributing to both our psychological and physical well-being. To embrace and sustain a constructive self-talk routine, it is essential for your thoughts to embody the following ten characteristics:

Realistic and Balanced: Healthy self-talk involves acknowledging both positive and negative aspects of a situation in a balanced manner. Adopting a realistic and balanced perspective avoids the cognitive distortion (i.e., thoughts that lead to an irrational or inaccurate view of reality) that often lead to catastrophizing or overly negative thinking.

Encouraging and Supportive: Instead of being critical or judgmental toward your inner thoughts, healthy self-talk offers support and encouragement that recognizes efforts and progress no matter how small.

Solution-Oriented: Rather than dwelling on problems, healthy self-talk focuses on finding solutions. Embracing solution-oriented self-talk helps promote a proactive and problem-solving mindset.

Self-Compassion: Healthy self-talk includes self-compassion and understanding. It acknowledges that you will (like everyone in the world) make mistakes and experience challenges, and that these are opportunities for growth.

Mindfulness: Being aware of your thoughts and feelings in the present moment is essential for healthy self-talk. Mindfulness helps in identifying and redirecting negative thoughts.

Constructive Criticism: When self-criticism is necessary, healthy self-talk frames it in a constructive and growth-oriented manner. This is key to emphasizing the learning and improvement rather than dwelling on mistakes.

Optimism: A positive and optimistic outlook, even in challenging situations, can contribute to healthy self-talk. The ability to view the opportunities within the difficulties helps foster hope for the future.

Empowerment: Healthy self-talk is empowering by reinforcing a sense of control and agency over your life. It fosters high self-efficacy—the belief in your ability to overcome challenges.

Gratitude: Incorporating gratitude into self-talk involves recognizing and appreciating the positive aspects of your life. Gratitude shifts focus away from what is lacking to what is present and valuable.

Positive Affirmations: These encouraging and uplifting statements focus on your strengths and capabilities rather than weaknesses and faults. The process of affirming yourself through positive affirmations is a powerful way to challenge your thinking, create a positive mindset, boost self-esteem, and change your negative limiting thoughts into more positive ones.

Psychology of the voice states that your voice is your most powerful tool for self-expression and affirmation. Your voice can shape your reality, influence others, and create positive change in the world. **When you use your voice to affirm yourself through positive affirmations, you harness its full potential to transform your life and the lives of those around you.**

In my clinical practice, I use mirror work in combination with positive affirmations as a tool to harness the power within—the power in the voice. I encourage you to start by speaking your affirmations out loud. The more you practice this skill of giving your affirmations voice, the more you will speak with confidence and conviction. Repeat them daily, either in front of a mirror or during moments of self-reflection. As you do this, pay attention to how your body responds to the words you are saying. Notice any shifts in your energy, thoughts, mood, or mindset. Over time, you will begin to internalize these affirmations, rewiring your brain for positivity, clarity, and positive self-belief.

And this is just the beginning! I encourage you to use your voice to advocate for yourself and others in all areas of your life. Speak up in meetings, assert your boundaries in relationships, and stand up for what you believe in. By using your voice authentically and assertively, you affirm your own worth and empower others to do the same.

Remember, your voice reflects your innermost thoughts, feelings, and values. When you use it to affirm yourself through positive affirmations, you not only boost your self-esteem and confidence, but you also inspire others to do the same. So, embrace the power of your voice and let it be a force for positive change in your life and in the world.

Your story is one of the most powerful ways to leave a legacy and to make an impact. **One of the most impactful aspects of affirming yourself through positive affirmations is recognizing the power of your own narrative.** Your story is unique; it is filled with experiences, challenges, triumphs, and growth. By sharing your story, you affirm yourself and inspire and empower others.

Think about the moments in your life when you have faced adversity and emerged stronger. Much like me and the story I shared, you may face adversity that completely changes the trajectory of your life. These moments are not just personal victories; they are testaments to your resilience and strength. When we share our experiences with others, we offer them hope and encouragement. We show others they are not alone in their struggles and that there is light in their future.

Sharing your story also allows you to connect with others on a deeper level. It fosters empathy and understanding, breaks down barriers, and builds bridges between people from different walks of life in different corners of the world. When you open up about your experiences, you invite others to do the same, creating a supportive community where everyone feels seen, heard, loved, and valued.

Moreover, sharing your story is a powerful act of self-affirmation. It requires courage and vulnerability to speak up and share your truth, and in doing so, you reaffirm your own worth and resilience. You declare to yourself and to the world that you are not defined by your past or by your circumstances but by the strength and courage with which you face them.

My aunt died before she had the opportunity to share her story. Her death is a part of my story. Sharing this part of my story with you has been both a difficult and empowering experience. Everything I have spoken about with you comes from both my personal experiences and professional expertise. I share this with you because I have lived it and have embodied it, and understanding the power of mindset has changed my life. I want the same for you. I want you to live a big and bold life, a life where you are not afraid to share your story.

STAND IN YOUR TRUTH AND SHARE YOUR STORY.

Self-talk is more than "TikTok therapy," it is the foundation of your story. By utilizing the 3 C's, you are ensuring that the foundation of your mind remains solid and anchored. By embracing the power of self-talk and affirming the strength of your voice, you will own your power and find your confidence to tell your story. Whether it is through writing, speaking, or having meaningful conversations with those around you, your voice matters. Your experiences have the power to inspire, uplift, and empower others.

In the symphony of life, your voice is the melody that resonates with the universe, harmonizing the chords of purpose, power, and positivity. So, let your words echo with the strength of your convictions, knowing that in finding your voice, you illuminate a path for others to find theirs. Your voice, your story, and your truth are the legacy you leave behind—a testament to your courage and a beacon for others. Go forth boldly, speak with unwavering confidence, and let the world be transformed by the power of your voice.

Chapter
NINE

CREATING CLARETY BY PLUNGING INTO THE COLD

To my mum, my entrepreneurial inspiration and an English Channel swimmer, and to my family for championing my passion for cold dipping. Special shout-out to my community of LOLOs for always holding me up and supporting me in doing hard things.

CLARE MITCHELL

For the last twenty-plus years, Clare Mitchell has been a public servant by day and a facilitator and coach by night and on weekends. Harnessing her passion and expertise, she creates engaging and brave spaces for individuals and organizations to "clarefy" what is important to them. Clare is always learning and trying new things, and she is fascinated by the mind–body connection, especially the power of the stories we have on repeat in our heads and how we can let them define us. With the right tools and know-how, she helps clients reframe their stories to serve their passions. As a certified SHERPA Breath & Cold facilitator, Clare loves holding others' hands, literally and figuratively, as they plunge into breath work and intentional cold immersion for self-discovery and the myriads of mental and physical benefits. Clare is married and a mum to two children, and the fab four love to explore Toronto on their bikes and public transit, as long as there is an ice cream store en route.

www.creatingclarety.com

@creatingclarety

IMMERSING MYSELF IN COLD WATER SETS ME UP FOR SUCCESS WITH MORE "CLARETY" IN THE REST OF MY LIFE.

@creatingclarety

Thanksgiving Monday, 6:15 a.m. It was cold and dark, and I was joining a group of strangers to wade into the even darker waters of Lake Ontario . . . because someone said it was hard and I might like it. Just follow the path, they said, and you will find the women. So I did, and thus began my intentional cold immersion journey.

I had no idea what to expect (except that it would be cold). I thought going into the water in October couldn't be that hard, but I was wrong, and thankfully so! As I dipped my toes in, it felt cold, then as I timidly waded in to my chest, I literally felt my breath being sucked out of me. It reminded me of the feeling you get when standing on the edge of something terrifying, like the ledge before ziplining. Your harness has been double-checked and now all you need to do is step off the platform. You want to, but you are scared, and the longer you stand there, the more your heart races as your brain plays tug-of-war: *Should I do it? I can't do it. Can I do it? I am scared to do it. I want to do it.* It's the push and pull of fear and fearlessness simultaneously sparring in your brain and body.

It was terrifying, and I panicked. My entire body tensed up as I gasped for air in shallow gulps. I don't know what I expected, but it wasn't this. All thoughts vanished from my mind. I couldn't even fathom that

I might not survive. My mind was blank, absolutely blank. I couldn't hear anything around me—it was like I was in a gigantic deprivation cone where my senses couldn't function. It was all I could do to breathe just to stay alive. And then, almost instantly, my fight-or-flight response kicked in and my entire being roared at me to get out. After what seemed like minutes, but was probably less than ten seconds, I tuned into the reassuring murmurings of the women whose hands I was squeezing. Their gentle reassurance reminded me to breathe. Just breathe. Their unwavering belief that I could do it, combined with my ego, kept me in the ice-cold water.

My toes were tingling, like I was stepping on pins and needles, and I felt as if I were moving in molasses. The hair on my body stood on end, and it was as though my body had gone into shock. Ironically, my skin felt on fire, frozen by the cold water in an almost uncomfortable way. It could have been seconds or minutes that I stood there; I couldn't tell.

And then it happened. The switch. I was euphoric and exhilarated as I realized I was neck-deep in ice-cold water, in Lake Ontario, the sun rising on the horizon, surrounded by this community of women who were physically and mentally supporting me, in October. A sense of calm like I had never experienced fell over my body, and my breathing slowed down and regulated. My panicky shallow breaths were replaced with calming inhalations through my nostrils. I was doing it. I was doing that hard thing I didn't think I could do. I wanted more.

For me, after the initial shock that lessens more and more as I practice, intentional cold immersion floods my body with that sense of calm each time. While I know I am immersed in freezing water, it doesn't feel cold. **And in this state, my mind is calmed. It can't spiral into those anxious places**. It must focus on my breathing to keep me alive. And over time as I have deepened my practice, the time it takes to reach this euphoric state of calm has shortened immensely. I still experience that initial shock of losing my breath, but it no longer terrifies me—it means I am doing that hard thing again. My body is becoming faster at adapting to this hard thing I do regularly now.

As women donning ever-evolving hats—as a parent, partner, friend, daughter, sister, colleague, caregiver, etc.—we never seem to have enough hours in the day for every role. But we are led to believe by the rampant images and messages bombarding us that we can have it all. And that we should want it all. Yes, it will be hard, but we can do it. And if we don't have it all and dare to complain about wanting more, then we are viewed as inherently flawed and not working hard enough. This constant bombardment, both subtle and overt, is like a soundtrack stuck on repeat in my head. As a mum to two, wife to one, and carer for aging family members who works full-time and owns a facilitation and coaching business, I do hard things every day. I hypnobirthed my two children into this world. I can facilitate a day-long strategic planning session for more than two hundred executives. I have run five marathons. Yet despite these hard-earned achievements, like many women, I struggle with feeling ambushed from every direction to do more. After all, I should be able to do more now. And here is the kicker: regularly being in this state of increased adrenaline, I rarely feel as though I am giving anything 100 percent of my attention in any given moment. My mind has already leaped to the next thing on my never-ending to-do list. The constant underlying anxiety of what else needs to be done invades my thoughts at all hours of the day (and night). It is as though I am in a constant fight-or-flight state. When something as trivial as forgetting to mark down an upcoming kid's birthday on the calendar inevitably occurs, I feel all the feels—anger, frustration, resentment, and more (you can fill in the blanks). Ultimately, I spiral into feeling anxious and want to throw my hands in the air and have my own temper tantrum.

Having survived two rounds of postpartum depression and anxiety, I am keenly aware of how quickly my thoughts can shift and taint my reality. Couple this with imminent perimenopause, and my mind and body often feel as though they are working against me, on their own agenda, and I am merely along for the (bumpy) ride.

WHY TAKE THE (COLD) PLUNGE?

In our bodies, the sympathetic nervous system (SNS) and parasympathetic nervous system (PNS) are two branches of the autonomic nervous system responsible for involuntary bodily functions depending on whether we are in fight-or-flight (SNS) or rest-and-digest (PNS) responses. In situations where we think our body is stressed or in danger, the SNS prepares the body for action by releasing adrenaline, increasing our heart rate, and boosting the flow of oxygenated blood to the muscles. It prepares us for action while suppressing nonessential functions like digestion.

When you plunge into ice-cold water, your mind and body think you are in danger. Your body can only take short breaths, predominantly through your mouth, and your muscles tense. The increase in adrenaline gives you an overwhelming need to get the heck out of the water. Once the perceived danger is gone, however, the PNS counterbalances the effects of your body's fight-or-flight response. The rest-and-digest phase that follows promotes relaxation and recovery by conserving your energy, slowing your heart rate, and enhancing your body's ability to repair, improve immune function, and restore the internal balance, thus giving you a sense of calm.

As Kristin Weitzel, founder of SHERPA Breath & Cold shares, "The choice to immerse yourself in ice-cold water for a short period of time can act as a hormetic stressor, a type of mild stress that can trigger beneficial responses in the body. Based on the context of the person stepping into the cold, specific protocols are used to create the minimum effective dose of stress their body needs to build improved cellular health, mental well-being, and resiliency. As we learn to navigate the icy waters by using our breath to manage and calm our nervous system response in what can feel like chaos, we begin to parallel this to how we handle challenges in general."

Kristin often reminds us, "**We don't get in ice baths to get good at taking ice baths—we get in an ice bath to get good at life!** By not only deliberately getting into cold but practicing neck-deep cold plunging with intention, people who use this practice begin to realize and step boldly into their greatest capacity as humans."

In small amounts, the little bit of imbalance these stressors cause is just enough to knock us out of our homeostatic zone, thus causing a parasympathetic rebound while increasing our resiliency to future stressors, releasing feel-good hormones like dopamine, reducing inflammation, and supporting elimination of toxins while activating a variety of cellular mechanisms.

Thanks to evolution, our bodies rightly know that staying in ice-cold water for an extended period of time can cause hypothermia and result in death. But the right dose is just enough to knock us out of homeostasis and kick in processes that make us better adapted at handling stress. With repeated intentional cold immersion, there can be an increased ability of the parasympathetic system to restore balance, which leads to potential relaxation and adaptive responses.

Doing hard things regularly can help us better respond to the inevitable stressful situations that are lurking around the corner. Being in a constant state of fight or flight (or thinking you are) eventually wears down the body's natural defenses. We are surrounded by micro stressors every day that cause anxiety and send us into fight-or-flight mode. For example, when an(other) online meeting goes too long and we know we are going to be late for an appointment, or when we take just an extra moment to do something and our child spirals into a meltdown. These stressors cause our heart to race and our blood pressure to rise; we feel light-headed and start to sweat. Many of these same symptoms occur when we initially immerse our bodies in freezing water.

I would be exaggerating if I claimed that intentional cold immersion has made me completely and calmly capable of facing all the micro stressors in my life. But it certainly has facilitated my growth and realization of the physical and mental strengths I didn't realize I possessed. When my heart races or my hands get sweaty and I can feel my body entering fight-or-flight mode in response to a trigger, I am much better able to recognize it and use practical tools to reduce my perception of danger.

MY PRACTICE:

My intentional cold immersion practice has progressed from weekly cold plunges with my Ladies of Lake Ontario (LOLOs) community to daily immersion in a 100 L galvanized steel tank on my back deck between September and May. I start with some deep inhalations, then with a press of my timer and one smooth motion, I immerse myself up to my neck ensuring my vagus nerve is submerged. The temperature ranges from about -4 degrees C to +8 degrees. From the moment I step into my tub, I can't focus on anything but my breath. The initial fast and shallow inhalations through my mouth still happen, but they are much shorter now and are far more quickly replaced with longer exhalations through my nose. A sense of calm washes over my body, and I return to my grounding place, my anxieties no longer vying for attention in my head. I can only focus on my breath.

No matter rain, snow, or sleet, each day I honor myself and my needs to prioritize my mental and physical well-being. In the winter when it gets really cold, there is something primally satisfying about breaking the ice on the tank with a hammer before I get in. Even on the days I am feeling particularly unmotivated, the hit of dopamine that I know is coming usually is enough of an incentive. Like the initial challenge that motivated me, I record the water and air temperature, date, time, and duration. I hate interrupting my consistency streaks!

Since my first intentional cold immersion, I have come to rely on the consistency of intentional cold immersion to navigate some of the highest ups and downs of my life. About two years ago, my mum, after experiencing rapidly debilitating cancer, was placed in palliative care. Her death was imminent, but she was conscious and surrounded by my dad, my brother, and me. As she drew her last breaths, I was there . . . fully present in a way I would not have been capable of before. Just moments prior, I had been panicking as my heart raced, my hands turned clammy, my muscles tensed, and I felt like I was having an out-of-body experience. I thought I might pass out, and I wanted to be anywhere but there. More than anything, though, I wanted to be fully present to witness my mum's final breaths. I don't think I would have believed it was actually happening otherwise. As I consciously relaxed my shoulders, inhaled deeply, and looked into her clear blue eyes, I watched as she took her last breaths, and we shared a life-altering moment.

Intentionally plunging into ice-cold water year-round has taught me the value of being uncomfortable and choosing hard again and again. When I am neck-deep in water with chunks of ice stabbing me, I am forcing my body to shut off the cacophony in my head. I can only focus on my breath and the calm that comes with it. It feels like a cliché to write this, but a consistent intentional cold immersion practice has the possibility of motivating and reminding each of us that we can do hard things every day in any and all aspects of our lives.

HOW TO START YOUR OWN PRACTICE:

(If you are ready to take the plunge, please talk to your health-care practitioner to ensure it is right for you.)

Start slowly in the shower. Immerse your face in ice-cold water for as long as feels doable. It should feel uncomfortable but not hurt. At the end of your shower, turn the temperature all the way cold for the last minute. If it is a challenge, do it four or five more times first before progressing. If the first one minute is relatively easy, continue to work your way until you can accomplish a full two minutes and twenty seconds. Start on cold, bathe in a temperature comfortable for you, then end on cold. "Champions finish on cold" is often cited in the intentional cold immersion community because you will reverse many of the benefits if you end your shower with warm water.

Progress to a longer dip. Fill a tub or find a body of cold water and take four deep breaths. On the fourth exhale, wade into the water, staying no longer than two minutes and twenty seconds. Be sure to have warm, dry clothes to change into and warm yourself afterward.

The buddy system. And as my dipping friends and I say, "LOLOs never dip solo." Make sure you are always dipping with someone else.

Immersing myself in cold water sets me up for success with more "clarety" in the rest of my life. When you can immerse yourself (or parts of your body) in ice-cold water and embrace it and the many benefits it offers, what other hard things are you going to plunge into in your life? I welcome you to take the plunge and choose the hard thing.

Chapter TEN

THE HEALING TABLE

To my parents: Thank you for showing me that nutrition and flavor can exist in harmony and for making home-cooked food a priority. To my hubby: Thank you for being the best sous-chef, for being so patient with me during food photoshoots before each meal, and for being the most cooperative guinea pig. And to my kiddos, Zoë and Bodhi: Thank you for always cooking with me and being so darn honest when trying a new dish!

TANYA BAY

Tanya Bay grew up in Toronto, Ontario, after leaving Iran at four years of age. In Ontario, she taught kids yoga, managed events at a science museum, and served as a Toronto Police auxiliary sergeant, then traveled extensively in search of adventure and new exotic cuisine. Global experiences led to an education in nutrition and food and falling in love. Her husband stole her heart while wrestling a 250 lb Blue Marlin. They traveled on yachts as a captain and chef team for almost a decade before settling down with kids. The gravitational pull of family found them back in Toronto where Tanya painted and translated her first children's book, a bilingual (English/Persian) nursery rhyme about a hatching baby chick. Its focus is on overcoming obstacles and celebrating achievements (ZoeTupeloBooks.com). Her expertise as a chef, nutrition training, hours cooking with her kids, and her personal plant-based journey has proved invaluable to her as a nutrition coach where she eases families into plant-based, nutrient-rich eating for an optimal healthy start. She lives with her husband and children in Toronto and shares recipes and tips on her website.

www.ChefTanyaBay.com @ChefTanyaBay

THE PATH TO A LONGER,
HAPPIER, HEALTHIER
LIFE IS THROUGH HOME
COOKING.

@ChefTanyaBay

The kitchen is the place I go to when there's chaos around and everything is in flux. You can visit my website for a cheat sheet on herbs and spices for different cuisines from around the world. Creating something out of nothing gives me a feeling of purpose. At times, experimenting with new recipes becomes a creative outlet for me, at other times, a mindless, repetitive task (such as chopping or stirring) is calming and meditative. It's truly mental and physical therapy for me.

Making homemade chocolate has become my go-to when I'm feeling overwhelmed. It's the perfect escape. I started making chocolate for my kids as a dairy-free, sugar-free treat to bring to birthday parties and now, instead of feeling left out, they feel quite special.

Making chocolate becomes a win-win, as the creative process itself is very therapeutic. I merge the cream-colored cocoa butter and the rich brown cacao powder until they reach the perfect melting point, then whisk in the sweet, velvety date syrup before concentrating intently while repeatedly pouring the mixture into the cutest little molds—tiny hearts or fierce dinosaurs. The careful stillness of my hand as I fill the mold to the perfect level, without any over-pour, is my goal. **There is something very satisfying about focusing on a small, manageable**

task and seeing a masterpiece come to life. It allows me to be in the moment and to forget everything else. Although temporary, it's sufficient in pushing me past a difficult moment. For tips and tricks, please visit my website.

I adore cooking with my kids, but I prefer making the chocolate late at night when the whole house is asleep. The best part is that it only requires three wholesome ingredients from my pantry and voilà! A quick and easy recipe that is delicious and healthy and reminds the recipient that they're loved.

While working as a yacht chef in my previous life (a.k.a. before having kids), focusing on food presentation was my meditation—cakes and pies in particular. I would stay up late the night before our final dinner, preparing my signature decadent chocolate pie. My creations often resembled mandalas (circular and symmetrical). The word *mandala* means circle in Sanskrit, and they serve to aid in meditation in Hinduism and Buddhism. I was unaware these designs were coming out of me at the time, but in looking back at pictures of the vibrant contrasting colors radiating from the center, beautifully captivating, there is no denying it. Focusing on creative tasks such as these allows me to replace negative thoughts floating around my mind, and seeing the end result of a culinary creation provides me with a sense of accomplishment and pride.

Food has always been a part of my identity, which started as a small seed in childhood. I watered and cared for it, and it has continually grown throughout my life. I worked as a waitress and food expeditor during my university days, I traveled the world taking cooking classes, I worked as a yacht chef for almost a decade, and now I'm a plant-based nutrition coach, something that allows me to share my passion for cooking and help others easily add nutrient-rich eating for an optimal healthy start.

Growing up with immigrant parents from a culture rich in culinary traditions, I never saw a shortage of new creations being brewed in the kitchen. My parents always cooked at home. My mother made pickled veggies, breads, and yogurt from scratch. My father doctored jars of olives with pomegranate, walnuts, and herbs. Things haven't changed much in this department. My mother makes my kids sugar-free, gluten-free raisin cookies, delicious hummus, and vegetarian Persian stews (their favorite), while my father bakes sourdough bread with ancient grains, ferments black garlic, and pickles asparagus. Food undeniably is my family's love language.

I didn't grow up with expertly piped store-bought birthday cakes covered in brightly colored sugary fondant. Instead, my mother made cakes with wholesome ingredients and an extra dose of love. I have fond memories of the marble swirls made by the subtle sprinkle of cocoa powder and the huge spread of fruits and nuts that accompanied the cake. My mother worked full-time but had the energy to juggle it all with a smile as she filled our plates with deliciousness. Summer weekends featured cookouts in the park with the extended family. Mom's Persian green pea and potato-pickle salad was a staple, along with large handfuls of fresh herbs and skewers of meat and veggies over hot coals. These family weekends serve as a great reminder of the commonalities of the Blue Zones around the world.

Research on the Blue Zones has taught us that centenarians in these regions eat predominately whole food, usually plant based with occasional small portions of fish or meat, with a daily consumption of beans and peas, or lentils and nuts. They also walk frequently and have strong, lifelong connections to community.

I'm not sure if my parents cooked from scratch due to the higher cost of pre-packaged foods, the added nutrients of whole foods, or the love for the country they left behind—or a combination of the three—but

I can proudly say I am thankful they did. Normalizing eating at home with wholesome ingredients instead of frozen chicken fingers or fast food primed me for a lifetime of healthy habits. Although I consumed my fair share of drive-through meals during my teen years, leftovers from the previous night's home-cooked dinner were an equal match against the temptation of deep-fried junk. However, the marketing for fast food was so effective that it wasn't until well into my twenties that I became in tune with the negative feelings processed food gave me.

Understanding the role certain ingredients have on my body has allowed me to take control of the way I feel. Learning to use ginger tea to combat morning sickness, fenugreek to increase breast milk, and tart cherries to promote better sleep led me on the journey to food-based remedies. I recalled how my parents treated colds with white turnips and soaked quince seeds (later on, I learned that turnips are extremely high in vitamin C and are referred to as a natural antibiotic, while quince seeds are quite high in antioxidants and dramatically lower inflammation). Along with honey, this trio has become my shield for protecting my kids at the first sight of a cold. This influence on my little ones is noticeable; recently, they have started demonstrating their desired control over food and the way it makes them feel by requesting energy balls when they're feeling a little lethargic or sour elderberry syrup during cold/flu season.

These traditions and memories are passed down from the kitchen and dining table to aid in cultural preservation. And when we choose to raise our families away from our motherland, it becomes that much more impactful. **The aroma of a familiar dish gives us comfort and nostalgia and an emotional connection to our heritage. These gifts are accessible to our children if we choose to cook at home.**

If you don't have a strong cultural tie to a specific country, an alternative approach is to host a culinary tour around the world in your own kitchen. One of my first jobs cooking was on a twenty-passenger scuba diving sailboat where meals were served family-style. This job allowed me to experiment with different cuisines and techniques. To help with meal planning, I would pick a country and prepare a whole meal around that particular cuisine. Favorites included Thai, Italian, and Mexican.

I encourage my clients to pick one day of the week to try a new cuisine and give it a fun name like "Worldly Wednesdays" or "Map-It-Out Mondays." Encourage your children to get involved in menu planning, shopping, and food prep, then ask for a review after the feast, which could include taking pictures of your food, critiquing it, and journaling about it. On Mexican nights, the kids can learn to say *buen provencho* (enjoy your meal), or on Italian night, *cin cin* (cheers). If once a week sounds overwhelming, start with a monthly one. You can visit my website for a cheat sheet on herbs and spices for different cuisines from around the world.

THE IMPORTANCE OF HOME COOKING:

A Cambridge study (2011) reported an association between frequent home cooking and longevity. They found that "people who cook up to five times a week were 47 percent more likely to live longer." Another study published in PubMed (2004) found that "adolescent girls who eat quick-service food twice a week or more are likely to increase their relative BMI over time." Many studies display similar results that home-cooked food = positive outcomes (a longer lifespan, mental health benefits, avoiding obesity, etc.).

Cooking at home has a positive domino effect toward a healthy life. Grocery shopping leads to farmers' markets, which inspire many to grow their own produce. Thus, fresh fruits and vegetables are readily available to make smoothies or large salads, leading to more energy and clarity, feeling better, looking better, and living longer.

By cooking at home, you can reduce your sugar and sodium intake and increase your retention of nutrients (by buying fresh and pairing certain foods for optimum absorption). Cooking also encourages movement, engages your mind, and saves you money. For tips and tricks, please visit my website.

With children, the ripple effect can begin quite young. A memory we often reminisce about from living in St. Petersburg, Florida (where our first was born), was watching our confident little eighteen-month-old help herself to fresh herbs straight from the garden; Cuban oregano was her favorite. At six years old, she still has a well-developed palate with favorites like fermented garlic, arugula, sauerkraut, and bitter dark chocolate.

Frequent and varied exposure to flavors and textures from a young age (even in utero) is key to raising children who are open-minded about food. Since cooking and eating are sensory experiences, encouraging our children (and even ourselves) to take in the sight, smell, and touch of food before we even taste it provides us an opportunity to stay present and pay attention to our senses. We eat first with our eyes, after all.

Most of my clients who struggle with picky eaters admit that they do not eat as a family, and **the number one most effective piece of advice I give my clients is to sit at the table without electronics, and interact with one another, ideally at least once per day.** The side effects of this one specific task are astronomical. We all know how effective our actions are over our words when it comes to influences on our children. In addition, family meals that include a little playful fun help remove the pressure of "eating" for some children. Sometimes I encourage my kids to imitate a certain animal when they're chomping down on their food or to close their eyes and guess what food is on the next spoonful.

HOW TO START COOKING:

As the Chinese proverb goes, every great journey starts with a single step. Just start. Start somewhere, and start now.

Tiny changes go a long way over time. Play cooking shows in the background next time you're folding laundry or doing dishes. Take a cooking class next time you're exploring a new city.

Make your kitchen inviting and easy to use. Empty your oven if you currently use it as storage. Stock your pantry and fridge with healthy staples that provide a base, add flavor, or include extra nutrients (ideally, all of the above).

Plan ahead and keep a journal for ease in repeating a dish that becomes a keeper. Start with a recipe with fewer ingredients and steps. Next time you're craving french fries, challenge yourself to make them at home with cleaner ingredients: russet potatoes (best for crispy fries) and avocado oil (healthiest oil for high heat). Experiment with seasonings: turmeric, sumac, fresh squeezed lemon, and a little pepper on fries.

Treat yourself to a countertop appliance. A multi-cooker that can be used as an air fryer, pressure-cooker, and slow-cooker can make cooking easier and fun. (Note: Many are still made with Teflon, which is harmful and has been linked to certain cancers, reproductive issues, and high cholesterol, so opt for a stainless steel one instead.)

Cooking, like most art, is a skill that takes time to develop. Julia Child said, "No one is born a great chef; one learns by doing." Show yourself some patience and forgiveness when things don't go as planned. Some of my greatest recipes were created from a mistake, a missed ingredient, or a modification based on creating a dish with the colors of the rainbow.

Whether cooking is calming and meditative or serves as a creative outlet for you, I hope you find the time to melt into the joy of culinary creations in the kitchen. **One's love for flavorful food is contagious and passing on our heritage one meal at a time is a gift we shouldn't resist providing to our loved ones.** The path to a longer, happier, healthier life is through home cooking. Bon appetite!

Chapter
ELEVEN

HOW YOUR BODY LANGUAGE CAN BOOST YOUR CONFIDENCE

To my two beautiful daughters. I hope they see the beauty in themselves as I see in them! To all the little girls we once were, you are enough, just the way you are!

TIOMI GAO

Tiomi Gao is an award-winning photographer and the owner and creative mind behind Blair Ann Studios. She specializes in empowering women to feel beautiful through contemporary beauty and boudoir portraits. She is known for offering a guided photoshoot experience with an editorial twist for everyday people. Getting that perfect shot is her job, but making you look and feel beautiful is her joy! She lives in Port Credit, Ontario, with her husband and daughters.

www.blairannstudios.com
@blairannstudios

WE ARE ALL WORTHY
OF FEELING BEAUTIFUL,
CONFIDENT, AND
WHOLE—THIS IS OUR
BIRTHRIGHT, AND NO
ONE CAN TAKE IT AWAY!

@blairannstudios

As a portrait photographer who specializes in helping women feel beautiful in front of my camera, I often see that we, as women, struggle with the experience. Women tell me they would enjoy being photographed more if they only lost twenty pounds, were ten years younger, had a toned belly, or (insert every single reason to be not enough the way we are). The camera is an interesting equalizer because taking a portrait of a person is a fascinating way to ask someone, "Do you like the version of yourself reflected back in the photo?" It visually forces us to face ourselves, which often brings up insecurities, self-doubt, and self-image issues from within that reside in us all.

There is a difference between *looking* beautiful and *feeling* beautiful. In my opinion, it's quite easy to look your absolute best. It is effortless for me to package someone up according to the current societal standards of beauty and transform them into looking like an editorial from a magazine. I do this every day at my studio, styling my clients in beautiful clothes, fixing their hair and applying their makeup, and guiding their body in front of the camera to create the best portrait they have ever seen of themselves. It is not always easy, however, for them to *feel* beautiful.

And the desire to feel beautiful is as fundamental as our desire to feel loved. I often use the example of Marilyn Monroe with my clients. She is considered one of the most beautiful women of the past century. Did Marilyn feel beautiful? Did she love herself? I dare say no.

I have always been fascinated with the concept of beauty, especially growing up in Asia before the age of ten where the societal standard of beauty is extremely high. I remember spending all my pocket money as a child on all sorts of popular beauty products with the thought that if I applied them on myself, it would give me the validation I needed. It didn't. When I was eighteen and nineteen, I entered two beauty pageants and was awarded two titles. I thought that would give me the validation I needed, but it didn't.

Owning my portrait studio is my second career. I was a respiratory therapist previously, working with premature babies in the NICU by supporting their lungs. For example, when a baby is born prematurely, say at twenty-four weeks' gestation and typically weighing only 500 g, their little lungs need help. My role was to help support their breathing. My oldest daughter, Aria, was born ten years ago in the same hospital I worked in. We were shocked when she was diagnosed with infant stroke twenty-four hours postpartum and was admitted to the same NICU. The chance of this happening was 2.3–13 per 100,000 children. I almost lost my newborn baby, which was devastating for me. Afterward, I found it difficult to imagine returning to work. I had a strong, unstoppable desire to remember every single moment with her, so I picked up the camera to capture these moments and fell in love with photography.

My longing to freeze time was powerful! To me, this is the essence of photography: I love you, and I want to remember you for always. As I continue to look for love and beauty through my lens, I've come to realize this love isn't just for our children, our families, and our pets—most importantly, it should also be for ourselves: I love me, and I want to love the authentic and whole me!

Simon Sinek, the inspirational author of several books including *Start with Why*, plus one of the most watched TED Talks, believes that what we need most in ourselves is, in fact, what we create and put out into the world. I found this notion to be very true.

WHAT IS BODY LANGUAGE?

It wasn't until I started specializing in photographing women five years ago that I began getting a sense of the validation I needed to feel so deeply comfortable in my own skin. I found my own beauty in helping other women find theirs. I attended workshops on body language training to help me guide my clients to feel comfortable in front of my camera. I also watched my clients transform in front of my lens during our photoshoot; they would move from a state of discomfort with self-protective body language to a state of high confidence, leaving my studio with a hair toss over their shoulder and their chest high.

Beth, a client, was going through a terrible divorce with a narcissistic partner. The end of her marriage left her confidence and self-esteem in shreds. Her photoshoot helped her remember her power and beauty, and made her feel beautiful, sensual, and desirable. She sent me a photograph of her images proudly displayed on her wall. A year after her photoshoot, she messaged me to tell me the cascading impact this experience had on her. It helped her recognize her own beauty once more and believe in love after her divorce. It gave her the courage to start dating, and she's now in a happy and fulfilling relationship. I was in tears.

Judy, six feet tall, long and lean, came in for a photoshoot. When she saw her portraits, she became emotional and kept saying she just couldn't believe the photos were of her. She shared that over the past nineteen months, she had worked hard to lose almost 160 pounds. Being curvy was something she had struggled with her entire life. As a result, even in her new body, she suffered from body dysmorphic disorder—she'd look into the mirror and not believe what she was seeing. Her therapist suggested she participate in a photoshoot, as it would help her see her true self. We both cried as she recounted this story. Looking at her photographed images gave her the evidence her eyes needed to convince her brain that she's beautiful.

In the past five years at my studio, I have experienced countless stories like these, and through helping others find their beauty, I have found my own.

In the study by Robert E. Kleck and A. Christopher Strenta from Dartmouth College, popularly known as "The Scar Study," participants were told that the experiment was meant to observe whether people behaved differently toward those with facial scars. Participants were placed in rooms with no mirrors where a makeup artist proceeded to draw a scar on their face. After, participants were given a short glimpse of it with a pocket mirror. Participants were then asked to leave the room and interact with folks in the building. Just before leaving, the makeup artist told the participants that the scar needed some final touch-ups. Without the participants' knowledge, the scar was removed, and they left the room thinking they still wore it. The result? They overwhelmingly reported back that people stared at their scars and were mean and rude to them, attributing it to the scars. Yet, they had *no scars*.

As this study highlights, **how we think about ourselves has a huge impact on how we think others perceive us—negatively or positively—which may have very little to do with how others actually perceive us or how we actually look.** Intriguing, right?

Now imagine all the automatic negative thoughts (ANTS) circulating in our mind. *Not thin enough, not smart enough, not achieving enough, not doing enough.* What does that do for our self-esteem and confidence? What can we do to suppress those ANTS?

Close your eyes and picture something you are good at doing. Are you confident you will be good at it again? The answer is likely yes; this is contextual confidence. It's a fascinating concept because we are all confident at something, yet no one is confident at everything.

Did you know that it was once thought impossible to run four miles in four minutes because no one had ever been recorded doing it? In 1954, Roger Bannister broke this barrier, then many other athletes did the same. So first and foremost, we must *believe* that we can positively change our confidence.

The recent discovery of neuroplasticity showcases our brain's ability to adapt and change at any point in our life. We are able to change our views and beliefs, including in ourselves. According to Amy Cuddy's study and famous TED Talk, even two minutes of "power posing" can help put us into a more confident state. Power posing decreases cortisol, the stress hormone, which puts us in a more relaxed, abundant mindset that correlates with positive thinking and generosity. It feeds our self-esteem and confidence.

HOW TO PROJECT POSITIVE BODY LANGUAGE:

In essence, our body language not only cues how others may perceive us, but it also cues how we feel about ourselves. It is a self-fulfilling cycle. **The more confident and powerful you feel, the more expansive your body language naturally becomes and the more confident you look.**

As a result, others will start to notice and respond to this confidence. The cycle repeats.

Let's start with some examples of power poses you can employ to shift your mindset. In general, people tend to think they are more expressive in their body language and facial expressions than they actually are. So, expand, take up space, and don't hold back! Your posture is the single most important cue for signaling confidence to others.

The Wonder Woman: Stand with hand or hands on your waist, chest lifted, and feet parted and firmly planted on the floor pointed forward and straight. Think of making a triangle, which is one of the strongest shapes. A modification of this is the Superhero stance; it's very similar to the Wonder Woman pose except your arms are down and relaxed by the side of your body.

The Elongated Neck: Increase the distance between your earlobes and shoulders. Winners in a high state of confidence typically exhibit this posture, with their chest open and lifted to the sky.

The Steeple: This is another strong triangle pose (think of the pyramids). Making the hand gesture in the shape of a steeple conveys confidence.

The Firm Feet: Are your feet always close together? Think of that strong triangle shape again. Place them three inches wider than normal, and you will feel instantly stronger and more grounded.

Shake It Off: We hold tremendous tension in our hands. Release that tension by making a fist and then shaking off the tension. Relax them, then hold them loosely on your lap if sitting or beside you if you are standing.

Bonus tip—Zoom OUT, not IN: Many people are conducting more video calls for meetings, so it is important to remember to keep your camera at a height and distance that optimizes your body language. Set it up at least two to three feet away, so the viewer can see your hands in action. You don't want it too high or too low so you can't comfortably hold their gaze. When others are speaking, it is tempting to look at the video itself or look at ourselves, so remember to make eye contact by looking into the camera while others are talking and not at the screen. You'll appear confident and engaged, and others will view you that way. (Visit blairannstudios.com/project/before-and-after/ to see some amazing transformations!)

Likewise, by positioning something as worthy, others will see it that way as well. In a social experiment, a baker baked a cake and cut it in half. Half of the cake slices were priced at $5 per slice and the other half at $15 per slice. The group that ate the $5 cake slices said the cake was dry, too sweet, and generally not very good. The group that ate the $15 cake slices said they were perfectly moist, sweet, and delicious. I laughed when I read this study, but I was not at all surprised. **According to a study by Stanford Medicine, if we invest more in something, be it money, time, or energy, we are likely to value it more.**

So, on that notion, I'd like to propose that if we invest more in ourselves, we are likely to value ourselves more. This is absolutely true for me. **The more I treat myself with love and kindness, the more compassion I have for myself. This leads to a deeper self-awareness, trust, and intuition, and as a result, I seek less in eternal validations and live life with more wisdom within my heart.** I have a deeper knowing that everything I need is already within me, and this is a beautiful feeling! What can you do to invest more in yourself? What experiences can you honor yourself with to feel beautiful?

I am a mother of two little girls growing up in a world bombarded with social-media messaging inundated with unrealistic beauty standards. I write from the heart when I say I hope my daughters feel a deep sense of self-love and empowerment. I hope they can understand that it's all just packaging, a way of expressing who we are through clothing and grooming. I hope we can all be empowered through body language and experiences, presenting a version of ourselves to others that helps us fit into society. It is within our control, and if we've lost it along the way, we can find it again. We are all worthy of feeling beautiful, confident, and whole—this is our birthright, and no one can take it away!

Chapter
TWELVE

INHALING DREAMS AND
EXHALING HOPE

To all the future parents of children with special needs: the day you let go of what you thought was the perfect life is the day your life becomes its most perfect.

NATALIE BOESE

Natalie Boese is a Hypnobreathwork® certified instructor and a lifestyle and digital organization expert who empowers busy professionals to reduce overwhelm and save time by creating simple systems for their health, productivity, and planning. When life as a single mum to two boys, including one with special needs, began to take its toll, she turned to self-care and Hypnobreathwork to regain her sense of self and positive outlook for the future. She now nurtures other women in how to simplify their mindset, time, and priorities. Natalie and her two spirited boys live in Toronto, where she and Owen love walking outdoors while listening to Rhys' favorite playlists on a speaker attached to his wheelchair.

www.natalieboese.com
www.macmadesimple.com
@natboese

NOTHING HAPPENS
OVERNIGHT, BUT STAY
CONSISTENT UNTIL YOU
CAN GET YOUR GROOVE
AND LET YOURSELF
DREAM.

@natboese

I can feel the cold rush of the water as I reach for the pink industrial soap. The medicinal smell combined with the beeping of heart-rate monitors and emergency announcements on the hospital's PA system make me lose my sense of time. Have I been sleeping here for three months? Six months? I catch my reflection in the mirror, and I immediately close my eyes. I sigh audibly. I open them again. It's only a day visit today. I want to throw up. I want to close my eyes and hide. I want to be anywhere but here. How is it that more than a decade has passed since I walked through the dark, secret underground tunnels to Toronto's SickKids Hospital, yet nothing seems to change? My throat tightens. How much longer can I do this? My body hurts in ways it never has before. My Achilles is torn, my psoas is ripped, my back throbs, and my heart feels like it's been broken in a way that will never recover. But he's twelve years old, and he's alive. He's no longer seizing. He smiles, and he's so darn handsome. I should be grateful. But I am not.

Unbeknownst to us, our youngest son, Rhys, started out life with epileptic encephalopathy, CVI, and soon became non-ambulatory. He was G-tube fed, low toned, and cognitively delayed. He developed GERD and a litany of other issues to follow up on as he grew up. (Sorry for the acronyms. These are a series of medical terms I had never heard of before but soon became all too familiar with.) While I have never wondered why this happened to me and my child, I have wondered whether I am equipped to take care of my son until the day I die. I just wanted to be normal and have a regular life, with a loving husband in a nice house and two healthy kids. Well, I used to want that anyway.

It didn't take long for that perfect picture to unravel. After Rhys' diagnosis, my husband and I separated, and I began to see what the world looked like on my own. Before my boys were born, I imagined myself teaching them tennis and taking them to outdoor concerts and bonding with them about movies, books, and music. I wanted to spend time with my friends and their kids, maybe even go on those trips you see others doing on Instagram where everyone is smiling and making sandcastles on the beach. Most of all, though, what I really wanted was freedom to leave my house and run any errand I pleased; to get out of my car without heaving a huge wheelchair out of the trunk and unfolding it; to not awkwardly contort my body to lift a child out of the backseat and twist while I lower him into the wheelchair. I wanted to be able to walk Rhys up to the school gates so we could greet his brother with all the other kids and their parents after class. Instead, I would calculate how many seconds it would take to park the car, then leave Rhys unattended in the school parking lot while I raced to the front to grab Owen without getting a side-eye from another parent about doing the unthinkable—leaving my child alone in the car. Everything was a choice. Well, almost everything.

Sometimes we have to play the hand we are given, and from then on, we choose how we want to live the rest of our lives.

For a long time I was physically healthy; I enjoyed playing tennis and running half marathons. But then there was a blip in the world when everyone was suddenly tethered to their homes, as our family was. That brief reprieve when it was normal to stay inside every day developed into agoraphobia coupled with my body physically breaking down. Carrying a twelve-year-old up and down the stairs day after day without going to the gym for support meant I could no longer walk, let alone run like I used to. The weight started piling on . . . ten pounds, then twenty, then thirty. Within two and a half years, I'd gained 110 pounds. My outer body was finally reflecting the way my inner body had been feeling for years.

The future seemed totally and completely bleak and without hope. I don't think I knew how depressed I actually was. Looking back now, I am not even sure how I managed the stress of having a child with special needs during a pandemic. Imagine a child vomiting sixty times a day. By the time I had changed his shirt, he had vomited on his jeans. He needed one-on-one care for every moment he was awake.

Then one day I was on a Zoom call as part of my Inner Circle Mastermind. I was building my business as a digital organization expert and the founder of Mac Made Simple. My goal has always been to simplify things for others and save them time. Whether through recommending lifestyle changes or organizing Macs and iPhones, I adore finding ways I can make changes for the better.

That day the guest speaker was full of confidence and determination. Francesca Sipma, the founder of Hypnobreathwork®, was going to guide us to "breeeeeeaaaaaathe." I had tried meditation before by using different apps, but I always gave up after five minutes and didn't really feel a benefit. So that day I reluctantly thought, *Okay, fine. I am willing to try anything at this point, but I just know I am going to look silly.*

WHAT IS HYPNOBREATHWORK?

Francesca describes Hypnobreathwork as a method combining breath work to clear energetic patterns, hypnosis to rewire subconscious beliefs, and visioning to fire new neural pathways to create the life you want. She shared her own story of leaving her career as a high-level advertising executive in Manhattan to living in Bali and studying many forms of breath work, including Holotropic, ReBirthing, Shamanic, Wim Hof, Box Breathing, and more. This inspired her to create a new method of breath work combined with hypnosis.

Francesca asked us to lie on the floor or a firm surface and cover our eyes with a face mask for better concentration. Then we were to take two inhalations through our mouth or nose. We were to first breathe into our belly, then into our chest, and then exhale through our mouth. It's a circular breath. She repeated this as we began to find our rhythm. The session lasted just over twenty minutes, and by layering hypnosis with visioning, it allowed us to create clear action steps.

As I listened to Francesca's voice over the soothing music, my mind whirled into a flurry of things that needed to be completed, and my shoulders immediately tensed. Then moments passed, and I started to relax. With her prompts, I began to appreciate the beauty of my situation. I started seeing possibilities when previously all I could see was a dark cloud in front of me. I began visualizing how I could travel with Rhys on an airplane, something I had only done when he was a baby. I imagined connecting with the Make-A-Wish Foundation to get clarity on how I could have a family vacation in Walt Disney World. Rhys loves roller coasters, but I couldn't imagine waiting in long lines or finding accessible washrooms. The Make-A-Wish Foundation works with Disney to create an accessible vacation for a child who wouldn't have that opportunity otherwise.

By the time the session with Francesca had ended, I was in tears, and many of them were tears of joy. I *finally* could see a glimmer of hope. I wasn't sure I was ever going to take that trip, but I knew it was possible. And if that trip was possible, then maybe other things I had forsaken were also possible. **I had used my breath to clear out subconscious blocks and was able to tap into my higher consciousness to have visions of how I wanted my life to look, even with its current reality.**

I began practicing this method as often as I could. I found other instructors who were leading live classes, and I purchased a course that allowed me to practice on my own. Each session brought me more clarity and hope. I was beginning to see what would make a difference in my life, and it didn't have to be as *hard* as I had previously thought. I started by making very, very small changes and created a list of five things that were my daily nonnegotiables. As I describe them, I want you to bear in mind that I was at an all-time low. They might seem basic to you, but at the time I just needed something to pull me out of the emotional darkness I was in.

Each morning I wrote down the following five steps and then checked them off as I completed them:

1. Make my bed.
2. Do my morning Hypnobreathwork and journal.
3. Shower and put on makeup.
4. Drink eight glasses of water.
5. Take two 1 km dog walks a day.

That's all. I started with those, and I did them daily.

Making my bed made me feel like a champ because I was now "the kind of woman who makes her bed every day." Starting with something simple meant that no matter what, I always accomplished at least one thing a day.

The consistent breath work was giving me more clarity on what my next best action should be. Ten minutes of journaling allowed me to reconfirm what I'd envisioned.

Before starting this routine, I had been so sad that I didn't think showering really mattered. I no longer valued myself. Once I began making changes, however, I showered each day and added moisturizer, mascara, and a little sparkly cream eyeshadow. I realized that by taking just a little bit of care in the way I looked marked a difference in how I thought of the woman I saw in the mirror.

By drinking at least eight glasses of water, I was helping myself flush out toxins and remove negative thoughts. Things were starting to feel like a win.

My last item was going for two dog walks a day. Since tearing my psoas muscle, I could not stand up long enough to fold the laundry because of the pain in my back. Walking had become unbearable due to my undiagnosed medium-sized tear in my Achilles, and I didn't want to go. Not only did I avoid the pain, but I also didn't want people to see what I looked like or what I had become. But I still went for the walks, and each time I went out, I got a little bit stronger.

All these things soon became second nature. Once they were, I added new small nonnegotiables to the list, but the old ones remained. After they became a habit, they didn't feel hard. They became part of who I was now. In fact, I was excited to wake up each morning. I remembered who I was and how I used to wake up to catch the sunrise on my 5–8 km runs as I listened to my monthly playlists.

I was hopeful again. I began to read up on breath work and meditation, and I decided to apply to become certified as a Hypnobreathwork instructor. I just knew that I could not keep this all to myself and that once I had the tools, I could share this with others who were in similar situations. Stress and anxiety can do horrible things to our nervous system. They raise our cortisol levels, making it harder to sleep and harder to lose or maintain our weight. They create brain fog, ruin our executive function, and blatantly make it very hard to see the positive in difficult situations. You might not be a parent to a child with severe special needs, but you may be familiar with post-traumatic stress disorder, chronic stress, or even typical daily stress.

Harvard Medical School cites that breath work can reduce stress and the effects that go with it. But what is breath work, really? It is an experiential therapy using circular, connected breaths to access altered states of consciousness and clear suppressed emotions and stagnant energy from the mind and body. Breath work was developed by Stanislav Grof, a clinical psychologist studying LSD in the 1960s. Grof found through accelerated breathing to evocative music, he could enter alternate realms of the psyche to explore and heal childhood memories and experiences. Through the change of balance of oxygen and carbon dioxide, we activate different areas of the brain to create new neural pathways for deeper insights and heightened clarity, while dissipating the root of unresolved emotional charges.

The best way to get the effects of any type of breath work is to practice consistently in the morning and to journal for a few moments afterward. The more often you practice, the easier it is to drop into that hypnotic state where your thoughts and visions can flow. You might be thinking, *let's be real. Where am I going to find the time to just lie around and breathe?* I hear you. Sometimes I still feel like that too, but then I remember, if I set a time tracker on how long I have spent each day on my iPhone, whether it's texting or scrolling through social media, it surely would add up to thirty minutes.

We all have time—it's how intentional we are with our time that matters.

I found a doctor who could repair the widening tear in my Achilles by using platelet-rich plasma therapy, which required inserting a large needle up my Achilles' tendon and casting my leg for at least four weeks. I had to do this procedure three times for a total of fourteen weeks in a cast. That walking cast allowed me to start my dog walks, and they brought me so much joy. Once I mastered the walks, I decided I wanted to go to the gym.

I realized it was too difficult to get my cast into the leg press or leg extensions while other people used the same machines. So, I decided to go to the gym when it opened just before 6 a.m. At first I was embarrassed because I felt like I was just swinging the weights around and not doing what the old me considered a real workout. But like with the daily five nonnegotiables, I was consistent with the gym workouts, and I showed up whether I wanted to or not. Even a terrible workout was a workout, and I slowly began seeing myself differently. As a result, my regular Netflix and wine habit dissipated. My weight started to drop off, and I lost ninety pounds. Some seasons it was faster, like in the early days, and sometimes it was slower, like it is now. But my muscles are emerging again and so is the old me—no, the new version of me is emerging, the one that combines my history, my challenges, and my triumphs.

HOW TO INCORPORATE BREATH WORK INTO YOUR LIFE:

Who knew that something as simple as my breath could trigger a series of events that would lead me out of a dark hole and into a place of hope?

So, when you think of your life and you think about what you want, take some time for yourself.

Start with a quiet space. Set aside even a few minutes to start, then commit to doing it each day. Consider what your biggest challenge is at the moment and envision how you want it to look.

List your five nonnegotiables. What are the daily habits of a person who has the version of life that you want? Write them out and choose five to start. Begin with ones that seem basic but are achievable.

Review and revise as needed. Each night, review the list and check off what you were able to accomplish. If you weren't able to complete them all, write down what held you back and adjust for tomorrow. Make it simple and keep it short.

My original five daily nonnegotiables included Hypnobreathwork because it allowed me to dream again. Eventually, Hypnobreathwork became just one of my modalities for coping. While I no longer do it every day, whenever I need a realignment, I add a session back in. If I get too far away from my goals, I go back and look at those nonnegotiables. Am I still incorporating them? If not, I add them back in. If yes, I consider adding another that will bring me joy.

Keep going. Nothing happens overnight, but stay consistent until you can get your groove and let yourself dream.

All your problems won't be solved right away, but you will be able to figure out the most important thing to do today. And you deserve that.

Chapter THIRTEEN

GET OUTSIDE!

Colin, Wes, and Rory, being your mom has provided me with the courage and strength to follow my dreams, and I will forever be rooting you on to follow yours.

JULIA DONNELLY O'NEILL

Julia Donnelly O'Neill is the founder of Toronto Nature School, a thriving alternative education and recreation private school staffed by a team of wonderful and enthusiastic educators. She is an Ontario certified teacher with experience teaching in every elementary grade throughout the greater Toronto area, with many years spent as a teacher in the public school board. In 2024, Julia became a forest and nature school practitioner with Children Nature Alliance of Canada. She is the mother of three kids with whom she loves exploring the great outdoors when she's not teaching at TNS!

www.torontonatureschool.ca
@torontonatureschool

SIMPLY WALKING INTO
A GREEN SPACE CAN
LEAD TO AN IMPROVED
MOOD AND GENERAL
SENSE OF OVERALL
WELLNESS.

I invite you to pause for a moment. Close your eyes and think of one of your favorite childhood memories.

What do you notice? What can you see, hear, or smell? For many of us, when we think back to our most cherished childhood memories, they often include being outdoors. For some, this may be playing outside until the streetlights came on, biking with neighborhood friends, or swimming in the ocean with family. As kids, many of us innately felt calm and happy when we were outside. Unscheduled time outdoors turned into a chance to create, play, and connect with the magic of the natural world around us. Hours of fresh air and sunlight led us to fall asleep at the end of the day with a sense of peace and calmness.

I grew up having a family cottage where I was lucky to spend my summers outside. I fondly remember catching frogs and swimming in the lake. For me, the outdoors provided a sense of freedom and space to move through the world in a peaceful and unhurried way. Returning to the same space each year allowed me to build a connection with the land. I knew just where to step in my bare feet when I walked the path after roasting marshmallows at night, which ponds and puddles to check for frogs, and what trees came down during a winter storm, all of which were a healthy break from spending a school year indoors. As I grew older and changed schools, met new groups of friends, and faced all the trials and tribulations of being a teen and young adult, the familiar outdoor space of the forest and lake became the constant in my life. To this day I feel instant relief when watching the water or the dancing branches of pine trees moving in the wind.

When I became an elementary school teacher and a parent, it didn't take me long to realize that many children had not had experiences being in the forest. As a teacher in a "traditional" classroom, I quickly understood there is a deficiency in what our school system and urban lifestyle is offering. All it took was one long rainy day being contained with a bunch of five-year-olds in a classroom with fluorescent lighting humming for six hours.

I started investigating forest therapy and nature schools. I became fascinated by the forest schools in Denmark where kids spend a large portion of their time outside. Research shows these kids are happy, healthy, and engaged. Additionally, the fact that babies in Nordic countries are put outside in their strollers for naps appealed to me. I smiled as I pictured a line of strollers holding bundled-up babies outside in the snow, then thought of my own eighteen-month-old at his daycare who hadn't been outside for three days because the playground had been wet. From there, I looked into why we as a Canadian culture are moving further and further away from the outdoors.

In 2020, I opened Toronto Nature School (TNS), an alternative option to public schools as well as a great addition to traditional education systems. The goal of this school is to get kids outside so the magic of the great outdoors provides them with the immense health and emotional benefits we equate with being in nature. Our school helps a generation of kids move away from fearing the outdoors to embracing it by creating the connection I felt when I was by the forest, the lake, and the beach. **We believe that kids who grow up feeling connected with nature will become adults who have ownership over the environment around them.** We strive to instill in our children a lifelong love for the outdoors so they grow to be adults who value their unique ecosystems and spaces.

THE BENEFITS OF NATURE

A few months after opening TNS, we began hearing stories from our families that their kids were coming home feeling grounded. They were sleeping better, and parents reported their children would be up and dressed and pulling their parents out of bed on TNS days, which was not the case on the days they were attending their public school. Some parents reported that kids with sensory issues who struggled at public school were coming home engaged and relaxed. Children with ADHD and neurodiversities seemed happier after their time learning outside.

The goal of being outside, no matter the weather conditions, was difficult for some families at first. They'd ask, "But what if it's raining?" Well, we put on rain gear and go outside. We've seen kids terrified of mud and getting dirty develop a love of rainy days and puddle jumping. "But what about when it is really cold?" We put on winter gear and go outside. **We help families create a mind shift about being outside every day despite conditions, which is a new idea for many of them.** And ultimately, the kids who attend our program regularly have shown an increase in resilience. They are understanding that they don't need sunshine and perfect weather to be outside, which is an excellent metaphor for life. Happiness shouldn't be determined by everything in life being perfect. Our students and campers have now become troopers who don't question the weather. One day, when a new kid climbed the hills and got their hands dirty, one of our regulars looked over and said, "Don't worry, you're a nature kid now."

We've grown accustomed to spending our time indoors. We're driving instead of walking; we are sitting in front of computers and TVs instead of strolling through parks. So why should we be outdoors? What exactly is it about nature that is healing? Immersing yourself in nature positively alters your mood. **Study after study reveals that people who spend time in nature report better sleep, decreased stress, improved cognitive function, and better physical health, to name a few.** Like the parents of the children at TNS, we are aware that kids benefit from outdoor time, but how can we adults receive the same benefits in our daily lives?

HOW CAN WE ADD THE BENEFITS OF BEING OUTDOORS INTO OUR EVERYDAY LIVES?

You don't need to book a hike or head on a month-long barefoot camping trip to get the benefits of being in nature. The fact is, I own a nature school and the last canoe trip I participated in was when I was fifteen. Let's just say it wasn't for me. I distinctly remember sharing a bowl with another camper and washing a spoon in the lake, and while trying to portage a canoe with another tiny fifteen-year-old, I recall thinking, *My parents are paying for this? This is brutal!* Some people love these experiences and schedule their lives around these types of events, which is fabulous, but you don't need a total overhaul of your day to enjoy the sweet benefits Mother Nature has to provide. You can add nature exposure into your life by simply taking a walk in your neighborhood or visiting a local green space.

Start with a walk: As a woman with three busy boys, I know there are times in life when even taking a walk can feel daunting. I remember when my oldest was almost four and my twins were babies. I'd get one baby into a snowsuit, stuff the other baby into their snowsuit, start to dress my third kid in their snowsuit only to see the first baby army crawl their way to the dog's water bowl and dump it on themselves, thus restarting the whole process. When we'd finally get out the door, I'd bump my double stroller down the stairs, squeeze the kids into the tight stroller straps (convinced I might be hurting their private parts and limiting the chances of my one day having grandchildren), all to finally make it to the sidewalk to discover it hadn't been shoveled and I could hardly make it down the street. My goodness, what an ordeal to get fresh air! But we would power through, and soon enough my adorable rosy-cheeked kids would be laughing and having a wonderful time. Sometimes they even fell asleep!

A walk in nature can have an enormous positive impact on not only your mood but also on your overall health and life span.

Shane O'Mara, a neuroscientist and the author of *In Praise of Walking*, documented the effects of walking on your body. Scientific studies show that by simply taking a walk, you increase your creative thinking, slow down aging, and boost your mood. O'Mara writes, "Walking enhances every aspect of our social, physiological and neural functioning. It is the simple, life-enhancing, health-building prescription we all need, one that we should take in regular doses, large and small, at a good pace, day in, day out, in nature and in our towns and cities. We need to make walking a natural, habitual part of our everyday life." So, whether that walk is by yourself, a social walk with a friend, or even pushing a massive stroller of unruly toddlers, it will bring on benefits.

Choose the best time of day: As established, walking in nature can have a profound impact on your health. So, when is the best time to get outside? A walk early in the day has a positive impact on your sleep and stress levels. In prior years, when people were generally outside much more, their bodies' rhythm matched the cycle of sunlight, thus causing them to be tired at night when the sky was dark. In today's world, many of us are looking at televisions or iPhones before bed, which causes our internal clock to be aligned with the day and night cycles. For those living in colder climates, it is more challenging to go outdoors, no matter the time of day. Some people are seeking lights inside their offices and homes for seasonal depression. But before you rush out to purchase the newest special light, you may want to add a walk during daylight to see if it helps. Even if you cannot see the sun, the exposure to the clouds during daylight hours will help circadian rhythms, which may lead to better sleep.

Michael Breus, a clinical psychologist who has tracked many studies on how to improve sleep, says, "Every single human, just as soon as possible at waking up, should go outside and get at least 15 minutes of direct natural light." Walking during the daytime and exposing yourself to natural light helps to regulate your body's melatonin production. Therefore, while all walking is beneficial, you'll want to walk during daylight hours as much as possible.

Pick the greenest path: Although all walking is great, a hurried walk to a subway stop will not have the same effect as a slower-paced walk through a natural space. Simply walking into a green space can lead to an improved mood and general sense of overall wellness. In recent years, forest therapy, or *shinrin-yoku* (a term for forest bathing coined in Japan in 1982), has begun being prescribed by doctors in some provinces in Canada. These prescriptions are generally given to patients who are suffering from anxiety, high levels of stress, and other mental health issues. Australian researcher Jessica Stanhope published a paper linking time in nature to reduction in pain. "Green space exposure potentially provides opportunities to benefit from known or proposed health-enhancing components of nature, such as environmental microsomes, phytoncides, negative air ions, sunlight and the sights and sounds of nature." **Green spaces (forests, beaches, parks) rather than busy sidewalks have a more calming effect.** The forest is generally free from the busy city sounds that may keep you distracted.

Of course, we don't need science to tell us we just feel better when we are in nature. Just as I experienced as a child at the cottage, the forest relaxes us and gives us a sense of personal well-being. If you can put away your distractions and be in the moment during a forest session, you are tuning in to mindfulness. Using your senses and noticing what you can see and hear in a natural place can turn your attention away from your stress and worries. Listening to birds or watching an animal scurry can recreate the magical feeling many of us experienced as children while playing in nature. And in our busy and stressful lives, we can all benefit from a regular dose of fresh air.

Chapter
FOURTEEN

RECLAIMING THE JOY AND CALM IN YOUR HOME

To my husband, Michael, for your unwavering support in this one wild and precious life; and to our kids, Thea and Alden, for being our endless supply of joy, inspiration, and magic.

SOPHIE SHAY

Sophie Shay is the founder of CHEZ SHAY DESIGNS, an interior design studio specializing in kids' spaces using Montessori principles. Sophie's child-centered designs prioritize functionality and child development without compromising aesthetics. Her spaces are joyful and purposeful and inspire calm, creativity, and connection for the whole family. Since launching in August 2023, Sophie's design work has been featured on *Breakfast Television* and *CTV Your Morning*, in popular brands including West Elm Kids and Oeuf NYC, and on the website Apartment Therapy. Sophie lives in Toronto with her husband and two children in a calm and joyful home.

www.chezshaydesigns.com

@chezshaydesigns

YOUR HOME SHOULD BE
YOUR SAFE SPACE, NOT
ONE THAT ADDS STRESS
AND INDUCES ANXIETY.

@chezshaydesigns

Life can be stressful enough. Our home should be our sanctuary, a place for us to exhale and feel grounded again.

When my husband was unexpectedly diagnosed with cancer while I was on maternity leave with a preschooler and a new baby, I was doing all the high-functioning grownup things on the outside, but on the inside, I was falling into a state of shock and despair. We had just moved into our new home in Midtown Toronto. As I looked around me, I was completely overwhelmed by all the unopened boxes, clutter, and chaos everywhere.

WHAT'S WRONG WITH CLUTTER?

According to the American Psychological Association, our home environment has an immense impact on our well-being and sense of belonging. When our homes are cluttered, our cortisol levels are constantly spiking. For adults, it causes stress, mental fatigue, and an inability to focus. For kids, it creates overwhelm and sensory overload. And when you've already got a lot to deal with in life, your home should be your safe space, not one that adds stress and induces anxiety.

I have always been inspired by Montessori principles—where everything has a purpose and place—in the home environment. I had created intentional, calm, and inviting spaces in our last home for my daughter, who had just started walking at the time. Kids even as young as toddlers are sensitive to beauty and order. When spaces are designed with intention and have a sense of logic and order to them, it can help kids find their bearings and build trust, autonomy, and self-mastery. We can do this by removing clutter and distractions and keeping things simple. Grownups are not all that different.

We all feel more connected and at ease in spaces that are beautiful and have a clear sense of order, purpose, and logic.

My daughter took to the environment right away: fetching her own snacks and water, getting a towel to wipe a spill, engaging in deep independent play, getting her own supplies and creating art at her table, and even dressing herself for the day. It was incredible to witness. My toddler felt immense pride in her capabilities and loved being an active participant of the household. As for me, I felt calmer because I was no longer on point to fetch a million things for my child, and I felt more connected as well because we were experiencing and enjoying our home together.

I felt inspired to bring back what I knew about Montessori principles to our current home. I was curious whether the principles could be applicable to all ages, including adults. I desperately needed something that created more joy and beauty in the world, something that gave me some semblance of control in my life.

I am not a naturally organized person when it comes to home spaces. But with the Montessori framework in my back pocket, I was on a mission to create beautiful spaces and sustainable systems at home that encourage family members of all ages to take active roles in enjoying and maintaining their spaces so that we can continue to get more out of the home we're in.

HOW TO TRADE CLUTTER FOR CALM:

Set your intention. What would your life look like if you could reclaim the space you live in today? How would your time be spent differently in a home that's designed and organized with intention for you and your family? Hold on to this visual as we turn it into reality.

Declutter. We live in an era of abundance and constant inflow. It's a modern phenomenon. Families are drowning in stuff. The reality is, we can't start organizing our spaces without first decluttering. We need to remove the excess of stuff to bring back calm (and sanity) to our spaces and our everyday routines. Otherwise, we are simply shifting around our unwanted clutter.

I'm just going to say it flat out: This part is not easy! It takes time and energy. Progress may not even be linear. Go back to the intention you set to stay focused and keep motivated. It's going to be so worth it. I promise! Carve out time in your calendar to tackle one type of space at a time. Be ruthless with assessing whether an item stays or goes.

Marie Kondo turned the world into a decluttering frenzy over a decade ago. Her method helps you decide what to keep or graciously let go depending on whether an item serves a purpose or "sparks joy." She has since declared, in 2023, that her method of tidying is not all that practical for families with young kids, after having three kids herself.

I think we can still be inspired by Kondo's original philosophy. We don't need to get rid of everything or strive to be a minimalist. We should allow space for things that bring us joy—which is really the whole point!

Highly visible areas. To gain momentum quickly, I recommend tackling the most visible areas of your home first. This gives you a quick win, and the positive effects can be better felt and appreciated by the whole family.

Container method. This is the method that leans on a physical limitation. It is especially effective with kids, since the limit is tangible. If your kids are in their loot bag era and are constantly bringing home new trinkets, introducing a "treasure box" of a size that you decide can be a way to honor their interests while upholding your boundaries of what and how their trinkets stay and get contained. Anything that doesn't fit in the "treasure box" has to go, but it's their choice.

One in, one out. This one is effective with kids and adults alike! Think about all the categories that this can apply to (toys, cosmetics, clothing, shoes, etc.).

Ninety-day rule. Often, we hang onto things "just in case" (see point #2). But we are sacrificing our peace and sanity when we let these "just in case" items take over our space. If you don't foresee yourself using something in the next ninety days, it's time to let it go.

Time for a pep talk for common mental roadblocks!

1. "My family members are resistant to this whole thing." Maybe your partner is not on board, or you're having trouble convincing your little ones to get rid of their twenty stuffies. It's important to be respectful of our family members, as this is their home as well. Don't get rid of their stuff when they're not home. That's going to break trust. Work through your own items first. Share why you're doing it. Let them experience how the change looks and feels. They may be inspired to get on board or follow your lead and do it themselves!

2. "What if I need it later?" is a dangerous phrase. We need to get rid of those "what ifs" to make real progress. Yes, life is going to happen. You're going to need different things at different times, but that doesn't mean you need to be fully stocked and ready to go to take care of every possible scenario. If you don't foresee using something in the near future (let's say the next ninety days), then get rid of it. This rule goes for what I call "our fantasy life" as well. Maybe you stocked up on lots of baby travel gear with the thought that you'd be one of those cute families who travel the world with their babies (guilty!) or you've held on to clothes that no longer fit properly (also guilty!). That's not your life today. Our home is not meant to stock every item you may need in the future just for the possibility of something happening. Our home is meant for the life we are living now.

3. "It feels so wasteful to get rid of all of this." I get it. You or someone else spent hard-earned money on this item, and it feels wasteful to get rid of it. But the financial waste already happened when the item was purchased (also known as a "sunk cost"). Now

you get to choose whether to pass it along to another family who could benefit from the item or learn to let go of the guilt of getting rid of something if it's broken and cannot be donated. Your calm and sanity are worth more than hanging on to these unwanted physical items taking up space in your home.

4. "I'm too attached to my things." We don't need to get rid of the things that bring us joy and are important to us. But we need to be careful about what we're keeping because it's easy to convince ourselves that everything is special, that everything is necessary, and that everything is needed. For example, my clients come to me with their challenges managing their kids' overflow of artwork. They're all so precious, and they feel bad about tossing them. I tell them that the benefit of the art-making process already occured when the child was making the piece of art (read up on "process art" if you're interested). We can create select artwork displays around our home and let the physical limitations of those displays dictate what we get to keep, and the rest can be photographed and turned into a photo book or used as wrapping paper for gifts. We can absolutely cherish the artwork while breathing new life into them or letting them go.

5. "I feel guilty about things ending up in a landfill." This one plagues me a lot too, and it sometimes paralyzes me into inaction. But I've since embraced donating to organizations in my city as well as listing my items on my local Buy Nothing Group so I know they are going to a good home and are getting the chance to extend their useful life. This does bring us back to point #3, which is that the waste has already happened. The only way to

slow the cycle is to be more conscious about what we bring in. It helps to have a big-picture roadmap of the space we want to create (like the spaces I create for families in my design studio), so we can get it right the first time and we don't fall prey to expensive trial and error or other purchasing temptations.

Maximize function and flow. This is where the fun begins, at least for me, as a kids' space designer. I love solving problems. And to me, maximizing the function and flow of a space is a problem I love solving for families.

When I first assess a space, I take note of existing furniture and storage. I look for ways to maximize accessibility and flow, while adding functionality and aesthetics. Often, existing storage can be repurposed and optimized to better fit the family's needs. In other instances, you can get creative with furniture that doubles as storage. In our home, we love our coffee table that doubles as kids' storage for train sets, magnetic tiles, and board games.

I try to get things "off the floor" and onto the walls where possible to open up the floor space (added flow) and create storage systems on otherwise underutilized vertical wall space. Don't be shy about mounting things onto the wall, even if you're in a rental space. Make friends with spackle, and you can be confident you can patch things up easily when times call for a change. Otherwise, you'll end up with lots of "furniture" sitting on the floor, competing for the same floor space.

Build sustainable systems. The key to sustainability is to build solutions that work with the members of your family, and not the other way around. It's important to work with your unique tendencies to create a custom plan that will work for you in the long run, rather than prescribing a set rule of classifying where things ought to be.

Placement. When it comes to placement of items that are staying, it may be surprising to you that I work with the families to understand what their most instinctual spots are for an item, instead of defaulting to just the most logical spots.

For example, if I were to ask you where a pair of scissors should be placed, you may answer "the home office." But if I were to ask you where you'd look for a pair of scissors, you might respond with "the kitchen drawer." Then the home for the pair of scissors should be the kitchen drawer because that's where you instinctually think to look.

Sorting and storage. The Rainbow Method has been made famous by the duo Clea Shearer and Joanna Teplin on their television show *The Home Edit*. The method sorts belongings by color, particularly the colors present in the rainbow, and it is mostly a design decision intended to create visual flow. Unless you and your family can navigate your items and spaces by memorizing their colors, I'd suggest finding a solution that works with your family's actual habits and preferences, as well as creates the least amount of work possible for maintenance.

Reflect on the personality types in your household, as it can guide you on the types of storage and classification solutions that need to show up in your spaces, depending on the space and the main users of that space.

Do you or your family members need things visible? ("Out of sight, out of mind?" Try clear acrylic bins.)

Do they need to hide them behind closed doors? (Can't stand visual clutter? Try closed storage with lids.)

Do you or your family members need things to be grouped in minute ways? (Use a bin sorted by sub-group of snacks.)

Or do you prefer broader categories? (Try labeling a bin for "snacks.")

You, too, can take control and design your home spaces with intention. With these simple steps and a new way of looking at systems that work for the whole family, you can reclaim the joy and calm in your spaces today!

Chapter FIFTEEN

INVEST IN YOURSELF– YOU'RE WORTH IT!

To my three beautiful children who knew no different when we had no money, and who have learned to appreciate the value of a dollar.

KERRY RIZZO

Kerry Rizzo is a Chartered Investment Manager®, a Certified Financial Planner®, an award-winning investment adviser, and the owner and CEO of KerryKnowsMoney, an online financial education course for improving financial literacy and empowering women to take control of their financial future. She helps clients develop a better understanding of financial planning, investments, taxation, and risk, so they can alleviate financial stress and achieve the "sleep at night factor" we all crave. She lives in London, Ontario, with her husband and three children.

www.KerryKnowsMoney.wealth
@KerryKnowsMoney

LEARNING HOW TO SPEND LESS THAN YOU MAKE IS A SKILL IN ITSELF. THERE ARE MILLIONAIRES IN EVERY INDUSTRY, YOU JUST NEED TO LEARN HOW TO BE RESOURCEFUL WITH THE ASSETS YOU HAVE.

@KerryKnowsMoney

As a mom of three, along with twenty-five years' experience in the financial industry, I have seen many difficult financial situations for my clients and in my own life. To be clear, stress in life is helpful to a certain degree. It allows the adrenaline to flow when we have a new project or deadline to meet and gets us excited about a fun event we look forward to attending. However, too much stress in our lives can be a negative. Financial stress can increase risks to our health, including heightened anxiety, issues with our heart, brain, and blood pressure, and add additional pressure in our relationships. According to *Psychology Today* and countless divorce lawyers, the number one cause of marriage breakdown is financial stress.

Several factors can add to financial stress, including feeling overwhelmed with debt, having a limited understanding of finances, or ignoring money issues because you feel it's all too much. It's like having an untidy closet or a junk drawer we don't want anyone to see—we just need to decide to address the issue and not be afraid to ask for help. I have helped many people achieve financial success and live financially independent lives. Usually, we just need a plan.

About fifteen years ago, I worked with a couple who were self-employed and feeling the stress. They had a mortgage and some savings and were hoping to one day retire with $500K in investments, but they needed guidance. Over the years of working together, they have become much more financially aware, they have paid off their mortgage, they've bought a second home for their daughter (who pays rent to cover the mortgage payment), and they've accumulated over one million dollars in retirement funds. They still cannot believe how much more they have now compared to what they thought was possible and are so appreciative of the journey we have taken together to get them to this place in their lives.

So how do we make financial planning better? How can I lead you to new levels of success and happiness with intentional spending? **Having control of your financial health is just as important as eating healthfully or spending time with family.** It doesn't happen all by itself—we need to work on it consistently and make it a priority.

Your relationship with money can be impacted by your personal history with money, what your childhood was like, and how you saw your parents deal with money. Was money plentiful or scarce? Were you allowed access to money or was it denied? What were the reasons? Our past experiences shape our views about money, and it is very hard to change what we learned in those formative years.

WHAT IS FINANCIAL HEALTH?

Taking care of your finances is just like deciding to go to the gym consistently. It is a muscle you need to use every day to impact your life. It takes twenty-one days to form a habit, so what if you committed to closely following every dollar you spend throughout a month so you can catch yourself when you are spending on things you don't really need? I joke sometimes and state: "You really only *need* a roof over your head, food in the fridge, and gas in the car; everything else is a *want*." I am not saying to never spend money on wants, but we need to be intentional with our money, just as we do when we decide today is "leg day" at the gym because we are being intentional with our time and focus. Can we do the same with our money?

What does it mean to be an intentional spender? Does it mean having a retirement fund large enough to not worry about? Does it mean being able to take a family vacation every year? Every item we spend money on is a sacrifice. We may not see it in the moment, but with every dollar we spend, we are giving up the option to spend that money on something else that may be more valuable to us. As the saying goes, "If you do what you've always done, you'll get what you've always gotten." Just as you make goals in your life to work out or eat better, spending less and saving more should also be a goal.

The thrill you have when you run a race can be the same thrill you get from watching your savings grow over time. Saving a thousand dollars is hard. So is saving ten thousand dollars, or a hundred thousand, but once you get started and you reach those milestones, it becomes easier and easier as you see what a difference it makes in your financial future. Instead of worrying or arguing about money, you can be comfortable—and calm and a bit excited to see those balances grow! When the next crisis occurs, you'll be prepared. Can you imagine the smile on your face, the feeling of relaxation in your shoulders, and the sense of calm over your lack of anxiety when an unexpected cost arises and you're not financially stressed?

HOW TO INVEST IN YOURSELF:

When you decide to spend money on yourself, could it be an investment in your education to get paid more, could it be an investment to reduce costs, could it be tax deductible? When you do spend money, you need to have an expectation that you will see a return on the investment, just like a gym membership. When I spend money, I like to see multiple benefits to justify the spend.

The only ways you can impact your finances are either to earn more or spend less. Earning more could entail working toward a promotion, taking an educational upgrade required to advance, starting a side hustle, or keeping your résumé updated, just in case. Maybe a new job would give you a much higher income, despite being comfortable now. It is worth considering what the future opportunities could be. Would it mean being able to help your kids with schooling costs, helping your parents, or retiring early?

Track every dollar that leaves your bank account. Where is it going? Would you be surprised? Try working backward: deduct all your known costs (monthly payments, insurance, groceries, etc.) from your paycheck. What is left over? Then, as soon as your paycheck goes into the bank, take the remaining amount and move it elsewhere. Like a squirrel hiding their nuts, I hide that money in investment accounts, so I don't have money in my bank account to spend. I follow David Chilton's advice in *The Wealthy Barber* and leave myself just enough for spending money. Just imagine at some point that you lose your job, or your child or spouse is sick . . . make sure you are set for any financial uncertainty. Imagine the peace of mind you'll have when you know you can handle a major financial issue or that you can retire at any time but you decide to work because you like your job. Goals!

When I was a mom of three kids under five years old, I didn't have any extra money. I was working full-time in financial services for a large financial institution and was basically working for my pension. We had no additional money after paying the mortgage and daycare for three. There was nothing left. Once a year, the daycare administrator would say to me as she saw me come down the hall: "You are the winner!" (I had the largest tax receipt out of all the families in the daycare. It was not a title I wanted to have!)

The kids asked every day if we could stop for pizza on the way home in our used minivan (yes, I had a minivan). Heck, I even wanted to stop for pizza, but I had a mortgage and a daycare bill, so I figured waiting for the pizza would be twenty minutes and cost $25. Instead, I'd go home and cook pasta for $3. It took me the same amount of time to make, was healthier for the kids, and it saved me money, which I then put down on the mortgage. This strategy saved me fifteen years of mortgage payments!

Focus on the big items. A home purchase is likely the largest purchase you will ever make, and by the time you pay off the mortgage, you'll end up paying twice the price of the home through interest payments, so unless you can pay cash for a house up front, my advice is to pay that mortgage off as soon as possible. You can always access the equity later. Paying lump sums and increasing monthly payments, if you are able, can get that house paid off in ten years instead of twenty-five, saving you hundreds of thousands of dollars.

Pay down your debts. If you aren't a great saver, sometimes a debt makes sense. It is a bit of behavioral psychology, but if you have a hard time saving, maybe giving you a debt to pay instead is a better plan. I was good at paying down debt and saving, but the debt always got more attention.

And timing is everything. There are moments in everyone's life when there will be an opportunity to save. Low mortgage rates, kids finally done daycare . . . whatever excess funds come up, make sure you redirect them into aggressively paying off debt or aggressively saving, because that is your moment. Do not miss it as you may not get another. If you handle it well, you may be setting yourself up for a fantastic financial future, and not only for yourself but also for your family.

Improve intentional spending. Make a daily habit of recording where spending takes place, then evaluate it daily, weekly, and monthly. Create a new habit and block it in your calendar. If you have a significant other, have a weekly or monthly meeting to review (with a glass of wine and cheese preferably). Where can you collectively spend less and make more? Can you utilize gift cards, rewards points, discount or cash-back sites? Can you put off replacing items and instead refurbish or fix them? Can you use the library or the consignment store?

Make a yearly plan of spending and a wish list. Prioritize the list and agree with your significant other on the order. Realize some years you may have additional funds, while other years you may be stretched a little thin. What can you do now to improve and plan so a tough year or two won't affect your finances? Learning how to spend less than you make is a skill in itself. There are millionaires in every industry, you just need to learn how to be resourceful with the assets you have. This is imperative.

Teach your kids about financial responsibility. I believe money management is the best skill you can teach your kids, and it is not covered in school. Discuss money with your kids and teach them about your struggles, mistakes, and accomplishments so they can (hopefully) avoid some common pitfalls through your sage advice. And model the behavior you'd like them to follow. Introduce them to financial experts as they embark on their adult years so they have people they can talk to. Avoid becoming the "Bank of Mom and Dad," as it will not allow for the struggle I believe we all need at some point in order to then truly appreciate financial independence when we achieve it. We often need to be reminded that when we were in our twenties, we struggled, and the struggle is where the lesson lies. We paid rent on crappy apartments, ate Kraft dinner and Ramen noodles, bought used cars that needed repairs, and figured out how to pay for childcare on our own. It's easy to offer to help our kids, just try not to act too quickly. The fear of not being able to pay the bills can lead them to find a better job, improve their skills, and learn to not spend everything they make. It's such a tremendous lesson that helped us to do better, and it's one you do not want your child to skip.

Intentional spending does not need to be hard or complex. In fact, the simpler and easier, the better. We just need to be realistic. You need to understand where you are today, and where you would like to be. In thirty years, you could triple your debt, increase the chance of heart disease, stroke, marital breakdown, mental illness, alcoholism, or anxiety, OR you could take action today by making a plan now to get out of debt, save money, and develop a strategy for the future. Do regular check-ins and include other family members. Talk about money with friends or a trusted adviser.

One lesson I share with my kids and use myself is to ask, "Do I need it, or do I want it?" And if I want it, I think about the item's true cost. For example, that $100 top my daughter might be considering actually costs more. When you add sales tax on top of the price, as well as what you pay in yearly tax (say 30 percent), the top really costs almost $150 before tax dollars. When you divide it by your hourly wage, you see how long you'd have to work to earn that. For someone starting out, that cute sweater could cost you a full day's work. Do you still want it? Ask yourself, "Am I making the best choice for this dollar considering my overall financial situation today?"

Let's be intentional with our spending by knowing every dollar could be used in a different way.

By making these conscious choices, we are reducing stress, bringing calm to our finances, helping our relationships, reducing anxiety, and improving our physical, emotional, and mental well-being. Give this tremendous gift to your future self by investing in yourself today. All it costs is a little time and attention to your intentional spending patterns. I am ready to invest in myself and in my family's financial future. Are you?

Chapter SIXTEEN

PLANTS FOR A BETTER LIFE

I extend my deepest gratitude to my daughters, partner, and family for their unwavering support and encouragement throughout this journey. Without their love and belief in me, my dream of Planted Souls would not be a reality.

MARIA MUNOZ

Maria Munoz, the founder of Planted Souls, is a passionate advocate for the power of plants. With a background in early childhood education and a bachelor's degree in psychology, she brings a unique perspective to her work by blending her knowledge of human development with her love for plants. Maria celebrates the rich diversity of plant life from her homeland, Colombia. She loves to help people successfully bring plants indoors and grow confidently as plant parents. Through practical tips, workshops, consultations, and other resources, she is dedicated to equipping individuals with the knowledge, skills, and inspiration they need to cultivate thriving indoor jungles and experience the countless benefits of plant parenthood firsthand. She lives in Mississauga, Ontario, with her partner and daughters.

www.plantedsouls.com
@planted_souls

PLANTS MAKE US HAPPY
AND HEALTHY, SO WHY
NOT LET THEM WORK
THEIR MAGIC ON YOU
BY BRINGING A BIT OF
NATURE INDOORS.

@planted_souls

Imagine a lush garden or a green forest. Are you inspired to take a deep breath and smile? What if you replace that thought with a concrete jungle? Are you still smiling? Now think about how most of our daily environments look. Our homes are surrounded by other homes, sidewalks, streets, and buildings. And most of us spend our days within four walls, staring at a computer screen. We then hurry out of work and into some form of transportation that might take us past a tree or two. Then, we step indoors and hurry to get dinner cooked, kids fed and taken care of, and finish up by "relaxing" in front of a screen again because we are exhausted from our day.

What do you need to go through to feel surrounded by nature? Is it a walk to a park, a drive to a garden center, or a ride on public transportation to the lake? Why is it that most of us have to go through such trouble to feel close to nature? I know this is not the case for everyone. Some of us are lucky and have access to nature right in our backyard, but according to research conducted by multiple organizations, including the Canadian Lung Association, the reality is that Canadians are spending 90 percent of their life indoors, and for most, getting a few minutes where they feel in touch with nature is an activity that requires some time and planning, and therefore, is often seen as a weekend event.

We know that as living beings, it is essential for us to have this connection with nature. We are intuitively and instinctively connected to the world with which we have evolved. All these buildings, roads, sidewalks, and construction sites are human made. We were never meant to have any of this. They are destroying our instincts and need to feel connected to nature. So, what can we do to reclaim this connection? I bet you are expecting me to tell you to move to the forest to ensure you are surrounded by nature every day. No worries; I know that is not realistic, nor is it everyone's dream life. Instead, I want to teach you how you can bring a little bit of nature into your indoor environments.

The spaces you are already spending your time in can be the same spaces where you reconnect with nature.

Surrounding yourself with plants is an easy way to reconnect with nature. But there's no need to get your hands dirty by gardening in the summer, if that's not your thing, or going without greenery around you in the winter. By bringing plants indoors, you get to surround yourself in nature—in your home—every day, every season. And it doesn't matter the size of your space. Whether you live in an apartment, condo, or house, everyone can find room for a plant and reap the benefits. If you're into cooking, you could grow herbs in your kitchen. No garden is needed. And it's easy to incorporate plants in various colors, sizes, and textures into each room of your house to make it feel like a home. From lanky and leafy palms to sweet and small succulents, you can dig in and grow something special that suits your style and space. But house plants aren't just for decoration. They offer up so many benefits that go beyond their aesthetic appeal. From improving air quality to boosting your mood, indoor plants are like little green superheroes in your life.

And don't worry if you don't have a "green thumb"—I used to be a "plant killer." Every plant ever gifted to me always died under my care. Eventually, I just gave up and decided I was terrible at keeping them, and the thought of owning a plant never crossed my mind. But this mindset all changed one day when I saw the cutest little one in a plant shop. It had been years since I had owned a plant, and I just had to have this one! It was a pilea, with adorable round leaves that made me smile.

I felt determined to bring it home and keep it alive. I looked up everything I needed to know about it: what kind of lighting conditions it needed, how much water it needed, how it grew, and where it came from. I dug in deep (literally) and placed it in the proper soil mix in the perfect planter, then set it close to the window so it could get as much sunlight as possible. I made sure to create a routine with this plant, watering it every Sunday. I eventually learned its signs and could tell just from looking at it when it was thirsty and when it was not. I also learned that occasionally losing some of its leaves was normal—there was no need to panic and water it more or move it to a new location just because of a fallen leaf.

A couple months in, this plant rewarded me with its first baby! Fun fact: Pileas are known as "the friendship plant" because they grow new plants from their roots that you can clip off and share with those around you (or keep them and build a whole collection). Caring for the plant became therapeutic as I was actually able to see how my efforts were paying off. It was so rewarding watching this plant thrive that I'd worked so hard at keeping alive! It made me feel proud and appreciated. Seeing new growth right before my eyes made me smile. Every morning after waking up, I would excitedly take a picture. My little plant was getting bigger and fuller with new leaves, and I had something new to look forward to each day. Now, I am not saying there wasn't anything else exciting in my life at this point, but it was such a simple piece of joy with which to start the day.

My passion was ignited and I started a "plantstagram," which became a place to connect with other plant enthusiasts and share all my growing happiness. As my plant collection started to grow, my mother, who had always had the "I have a black thumb" mentality, was encouraged by my success to give it a try. We bonded over our budding interest, took trips to nurseries, shared cuttings, and watched our indoor gardens flourish. Friends and family who visited could not help but be amazed the appeal my many plants gave my place. They also joined in on the growing craze. The commitment, care, and passion everyone developed for these plants was incredible.

This passion for plants, coupled with my background as an early childhood educator, inspired me to start Planted Souls. My goal is to help cultivate a deeper connection between people and nature by spreading the joy of plants far and wide. Through education, inspiration, and innovative solutions, I aim to inspire individuals and communities to embrace the transformative power of plants.

WHAT ARE THE BENEFITS OF KEEPING PLANTS?

Plants give you a way to increase both your physical and mental well-being. Researchers at North Carolina University concluded that just the act of looking at plants helps reduce our cortisol levels, cortisol being the main stress hormone. Lower cortisol levels result in a relaxed state and overall well-being, so just by growing a few plants in your indoor environment, you will reduce your stress levels. I don't know a single person who doesn't want a little control over their stress! This same calming effect extends to lower blood pressure. Along with these relaxing benefits, plants have also been proven to quicken recovery time and reduce pain perceptions in hospital settings, thus allowing patients to rely less on pain medication.

Plants help improve our air quality. They literally breathe in the carbon dioxide we exhale, turn it into oxygen, then release this clean oxygen for us to breathe. Plants also absorb many of the toxins we have in our indoor spaces, such as those emitted from paints, cleaners, furniture, and more. Certain ones, like snake and spider plants, are especially good at removing pollutants from the air. In fact, NASA's Clean Air Study found that houseplants can remove up to 87 percent of air toxins in twenty-four hours! Additionally, plants release moisture into our indoor atmospheres through evapotranspiration, which helps us maintain humidity levels. By cleaning and maintaining humidity levels in the air we breathe, plants enhance our respiratory health, which is a great benefit for those with respiratory conditions. So, placing a few plants around your home can significantly enhance the air quality and make your environment healthier.

Plants make us happier. Considering everything we have already learned about our human need to have a connection with nature, it is no surprise to learn that plants have a positive effect on our mood. **Plants have been proven in several studies to lift our spirits, enhance our feelings of happiness and well-being, and increase our productivity and concentration.** Their natural visual stimulation, plus our connection with nature, help us stay focused on tasks longer. Just like plants increase our concentration, they also boost our creativity. Having a green environment stimulates our creativity and problem-solving skills, making offices and classrooms great homes for plants.

Plants grow responsibility. My personal favorite benefit is a plant's ability to increase our self-esteem and sense of purpose. Caring for these plants and seeing them grow and thrive from our care creates a sense of accomplishment, something that is hard to receive from many of our typical day-to-day tasks. Kids, especially, love having a plant in their room they can nurture. Get them involved by letting them pick their own (you can direct them to some of the easier-to-grow varieties). They can pick the color of the pot and even give their new "pet" plant a name. You'll be amazed by how involved they'll become. I run parties and camps for children at Planted Souls and can attest that they absolutely love leaving with their very own plant to nurture.

HOW TO BRING PLANTS INTO YOUR LIFE:

You might be inspired but unsure where to start. Just like I was, you may be intimidated by the thought of keeping a plant alive because you have already killed some. The good news is, you are not alone! I have helped hundreds of people find their green thumb and change their narrative from "plant killer" to "plant parent," and I am here to help get you started in a way that does not seem scary.

All you need is the will and a window. I always recommend my clients start off with either a snake plant (Sansevieria) or a Zz plant (Zanzibar Gem). These are my favorite plants to recommend to beginners because they are very adaptable and will thrive in most lighting situations. They do well in bright rooms as well as in low-light spaces.

Do your research. Stop into your local nursery or plant shop and look around. You're bound to be inspired by the gorgeous greenery readily available for you. Ask about options. You'll be amazed at the variety available for every price point and every comfort level. Find out what size pot is needed, the amount of light required, and how often to water.

Water when needed. If you're concerned with overwatering, rest assured that there are many easy-to-grow plants that are also drought tolerant, so if you forget to water them, they will be okay. The key with these plants is to actually take it easy with the watering since they are sensitive to overwatering. Less is more, and it is better to have them get a bit dry than overwatered.

Follow these easy steps, and you will have a thriving plant that will boost your confidence! Then you may even want to venture out and try another plant, and then another, until eventually you are living in a space with thriving plants that are helping you thrive in life in return. By giving them life, they will improve yours. Plants make us happy and healthy, so why not let them work their magic on you by bringing a bit of nature indoors.

Chapter
SEVENTEEN

WHAT'S BEST FOR YOU?

To my husband, Imran, my rock, teammate, and greatest supporter, and to our children, Sulaiman and Dina, the sparks of joy that light up our days. Thank you for reminding me to slow down and cherish life's little things. To Nas, thank you for standing by my side through this incredible journey. And Mama, thank you for teaching me to push through adversity.

NAUSHEEN HUSAIN

Nausheen Husain is a lawyer who has practiced immigration, family, and e-discovery law in addition to supporting women and families in pro bono cases. She chose to temporarily step away from her legal career to fully immerse herself in the journey of motherhood, a decision that presented both challenges and unparalleled joy, thus making it the most fulfilling chapter of her life so far. Nausheen is currently on an inward journey to live a more authentic, purpose-filled life, and she is embracing the happiness and alignment that comes with it. She lives in Oakville, Ontario, with her husband and two children.

@nausheengram

WE DON'T NEED TO
IMPOSE OUR VALUES ON
OTHERS, NOR SHOULD
WE FEEL THE NEED TO
JUSTIFY OUR DECISIONS
TO EVERYONE. THE
GOAL IS TO BE IN
ALIGNMENT WITH
YOURSELF.

@nausheengram

Have you ever believed you were doing something correctly but then a random comment from a well-meaning stranger makes you question everything?

As a lawyer, I've always known the importance of critical thinking, but as a new mother, I noticed my perspective was easily swayed by outside pressures and prejudices. Case in point: When my son was a year old, I had a casual conversation in a playground with another new mom. She was visiting from Spain, and our talk quickly turned to our young sons' sleeping habits. Her son co-slept with her, and my son slept in a crib in a room adjacent to mine. She went on to explain how she found it interesting that infants often sleep in cribs in North America, because in her village, infants usually sleep with their moms. "It would be considered neglectful if we put our kids in another room," she stated. I informed her that in North America, we are taught to encourage our children's independence almost as soon as they are born, and it is potentially deemed unsafe if they sleep in the bed with us, something my son's pediatrician had mentioned several times. I admitted that I struggled with my decision as I intuitively felt having him closer to me was more natural, but I had always accepted that putting him in a crib was the "right" thing to do. She laughingly admitted that she would like to have the option of some flexibility, but she wouldn't put him in another room since she feared she would be considered a "bad" mom.

That chance conversation stayed with me. Because we were on opposite sides of "the pond," we made opposite decisions about where our infants slept. We both were doing something because we a) wanted to be good moms, and b) felt pressured by society to conform to "the best way" of parenting because it was the expectation, but it wasn't necessarily because *we* believed it was best for our child or our personal circumstances.

It got me thinking. How much of what I do as a mom is a result of just following what society has determined for me? How much of it is what I've come to believe a "good" mother does without giving critical thought as to what's best for my family?

WHO DECIDES WHAT'S BEST FOR US?

I decided to temporarily leave my legal practice after I became a mom. The high-stress environment, adversarial nature, grueling hours, and intense competition had been affecting my health and well-being for years. I had changed specialties a few times and had found a fit as a contract e-discovery lawyer where I controlled my caseload and enjoyed the focus on analysis and research. However, I still felt I couldn't remain competitive and advance my career while also starting my journey as a mom. Something had to give, and I didn't want it to be my family life, since that's where my heart was.

I'm not sure what it is about motherhood, but it seems to be an open invitation for unsolicited opinions. When I announced my leave at work, for example, I was surprisingly met with a variety of polarized reactions. Some applauded me for my "sacrifice," while others alluded that I was out of my mind. "Why would you leave your career? You worked so hard for it. Are you going to just stay at home? For how long?" I even received criticism: "You must be lazy; you just don't want to work." **I was met with so much judgment for something I believed was right for my family and me.**

Additionally, I started noticing how much media reduced the role to "just a mom." It made me feel like my value was lessened in the eyes of those around me simply because I wasn't working for an income. I was grateful to be in a position where I could make this decision for myself, yet the judgment left me feeling inadequate.

Most of us have no idea what we are doing when we become moms. There are so many moving parts; there is so much newness to rapidly adopt. And as anyone with multiple kids quickly learns, every child is unique. We are incredibly fragile and vulnerable during this period, especially when it is our first child, and we are even more fragile if we are battling postpartum depression. If you are a mom who is too nurturing, you are considered soft, and your children will be weak and spoiled. If you are too strict, you will traumatize them. If you feed them only healthy organic foods, you are too rigid and your kids will rebel, but if you are relaxed about food and give your children candy, you don't care about your children's health. If you let your kids use screens, you are rotting their brains, but if you don't, you are impractical.

The judgment doesn't stop at advice-giving on parenting, it is also embedded within the societal expectation we put on moms at large. As moms, we are expected to "do it all": work, raise children, and maintain a pristine, organized home, all while putting ourselves last. The implication is that prioritizing everyone's needs over our own makes us good moms. Meanwhile, we are met with comments about our weight, how tired we look, how clean or messy our house is, and more. If you happen to mention that you haven't eaten or showered, you hear responses like "Welcome to motherhood; it's not about you anymore." It's no surprise that according to research done by Peanut (an online community that creates a safe space and support for moms), "75 percent of moms feel invisible in their journey and 94 percent feel unappreciated, unacknowledged, or unseen." This is a problem.

I personally found this exceptionally hard as I used to feel everyone's opinions held more credibility than my own. I would tell myself, "But they have experience and I don't . . . so they must be right. *Right?*"

I was suffering from "perfect mom syndrome," an overwhelming urge to get everything right but feeling as if I was constantly falling short. It's an extension of "good girl syndrome" where you grow up believing you have to please others and conform to societal expectations in order to be accepted. Your self-worth and security are tied to external validation and praise. It gives root to the belief that we need to appear perfect to be accepted.

When I became a mom, I felt immense guilt for not measuring up to others' idealized version of motherhood and how a mom "should" act. I created an idea in my head based on everything I saw and heard and who I told myself I had to be, and I couldn't keep up with it. By extension, I felt like a failure whenever I lost my cool, my child acted up, I made a mistake, etc. I felt like a failure if people disapproved of something I did. It was a lose-lose formula. But as I started talking with other moms and doing my own research, I've come to realize this feeling of judgment and failure is universal. I wasn't alone.

Where do these ideals come from? Some say it's from the widespread images of "perfect" women we see across the media. Actress and activist Jameela Jamil stated in her interview on the *Women of Impact* podcast, "So many of the things that we do, we do almost subconsciously. Because so much of the narrative that's telling us what to do is so pervasive, it's insidious. It seeps into our songs, and our TV shows, our movies."

I feel even more so that these ideals ubiquitously take shape in the casual conversations we have heard all our lives about how women should or should not act. Together, these expectations increase social comparison, which leads to the belief that we will never be enough. **When these pressures accumulate over time, we slowly lose more and more of our individuality and ultimately forget who we are and what we actually value. We lose the ability to hear our own voice.**

One day when I was on the verge of burnout, I finally decided to pick up Mark Manson's book *The Subtle Art of Not Giving a F*ck*. It came highly recommended to me by my best friend, but I was always turned off by the author's overuse of "f bombs." This book changed the way I view life's challenges. In his book, Manson talks about taking full responsibility for everything in your life. Not fault or blame, responsibility. "We don't always control what happens to us. But we always control how we interpret what happens to us, as well as how we respond," he writes.

I never thought of it like this before. I have a choice. I can't control people saying things, and what they say may bother me, but it's *my* choice how I take it in and allow it to affect me. Echoing Manson, we are making a choice "every moment of every day" about what we allow ourselves to care about. Change begins with making a conscious choice to drop it and care about something else. I agree when he says, "It really is that simple. It's just not easy."

So, how do you begin freeing yourself from all the expectations you've held on to for so many years? How do you stop caring about the things that hold you back? Admittedly, I am a work in progress, but the following steps have really helped me move forward.

HOW TO BREAK FREE OF JUDGMENTS:

Write out all the expectations you feel weigh you down. As Jamil tasked on *Women of Impact*, "You should make a list of what it is that you think your shackles may be, because often you don't recognize them when they are on you."

Get them out of your head, write them out, and give them a long look. Read them out loud.

Ask yourself what *your* actual opinion is. Next, remind yourself that if they don't align with *your* values, you don't *have* to apply them. What do *yo*u believe? What *do* you value? You may find that you agree with them in some part. For me, I wanted to be a stay-at-home mom temporarily, and it wasn't societal or cultural influence that made me want this time. Being a nurturer is a cherished attribute that feels innate to me. It's a part of me I celebrate wholeheartedly. But I combined this with the belief I had to wholly self-sacrifice and neglect my needs in order to nurture. So, I had to learn to accept the first part and reject the latter. I had to redefine the term for myself, shed external noise, and let go of my old expectations of what it meant to be a nurturer.

Figuring out what your values are may take some time. Journal your thoughts and see where it leads you. Meditation/prayer can also help. Ask yourself what works best for you, your children, and your family. Once you fine-tune your values, print them out and stick them on your mirror as a daily reminder. Remember, though, that you can change your mind as you learn, grow, and adapt to new situations—just make sure to gauge *your* "why" to avoid falling into the sneaky trap of seeking out approval.

You are in control; it's your choice to let it affect you or not. For many of us, this needs to be a daily reminder until it becomes hardwired in our mindset.

Break the cycle with your actions. This has two parts. First, work on setting healthy boundaries. This has admittedly been a challenge for me to implement, and I continue to work on it daily. I used to have a negative view on boundaries. I believed having boundaries meant I selfishly did not care for others. **What I have come to understand, however, is that it actually meant I did not care for myself. I now realize setting boundaries is crucial because it forces you to reevaluate your choices, protect your space, and value yourself.** Thus, it allows you to be a more loving, kind, and compassionate person from a more genuine place because you are no longer operating from a place of lack or resentment. As Brené Brown states in *Atlas of the Heart*, "Boundaries are a prerequisite for compassion and empathy. We can't connect with someone unless we're clear about where we end and they begin."

So, go to the party but leave when *you* need to. You may disappoint people and it will be uncomfortable, but it will be okay.

Second, **it is crucial to show up as a loving, nonjudgmental presence for others. Show others kindness, compassion, and acceptance.** Everyone's circumstances are different. What works for one of us might not work for all. I have made the commitment to myself that I will not offer unsolicited advice unless specially asked to share my opinion. Instead, I will listen and provide support. This is what we truly crave and will move us to learn to trust our own choices.

Practice self-compassion. Most of all, give yourself grace and remind yourself that to err is human. This is going to take time, as it's not a quick fix—it's a commitment to yourself, and a lifelong one. It's going to take frequently reminding yourself, and there are bound to be slipups along the way.

Make the motherhood journey your own. None of us will live up to being a "perfect mom" or even a "good mom" in everyone's eyes; it's a futile endeavor. Someone is always going to disapprove of something we do. And we won't always agree with other people's opinions. **Let go of all these conflicting expectations, reject the ones that don't align with your values, accept the ones that do, and live those with confidence.** We don't need to impose our values on others, nor should we feel the need to justify our decisions to everyone. The goal is to be in alignment with yourself. I believe once we start to practice this, we will begin achieving that freedom to be the version of ourselves we so desperately desire. Author Louise Hay put it perfectly: "I let go of all expectations. People, places and things are free to be themselves, and I am free to be me."

Years later when I had my second child, I took all the safety precautions into account and chose to have my daughter co-sleep with me. She is starting junior kindergarten this year, and I am ready to return to work for an income. If I could go back to that conversation at the playground in 2018 when the other mom and I spoke about societal pressures, I'd say, "There is no single best way, only the way that works best for you."

Chapter EIGHTEEN

DISCOVER THE POWER OF YOUR AUTHENTIC SELF WITH JOURNALING

To my parents, for their boundless love and support for me to come into who I am and to live a life without limits. You will forever be my greatest source of inspiration.

DR. STACY THOMAS

Dr. Stacy Thomas is an award-winning clinical psychologist, acclaimed speaker, and the CEO, founder, and clinical director of The Design Your Life Centre, a psychotherapy practice based in Toronto. With more than twenty years' experience helping people navigate some of life's most difficult journeys, Dr. Stacy's strength is in her ability to recognize resilience and teach people how to apply proven psychological strategies in order to move past mere survival so they can thrive in the face of adversity. She credits her own spiritual awakening and dedication to spiritual practice for being able to honor her authenticity and show up powerfully and joyfully aligned with her purpose. She welcomes the opportunity to help others learn how to do the same.

www.designyourlifecentre.com
www.growingforwardjournal.com
@drstacytoronto
@dylcentre

LIFE WANTS US TO ALLOW OUR TRUE SELF TO EMERGE FROM UNDERNEATH THE ADAPTATIONS WE'VE TAKEN ON TO SURVIVE THE UNCONSCIOUSNESS WE WERE BORN INTO. INDEED, COMING INTO OURSELVES IN THIS LIFETIME IS OUR ONLY PURPOSE.

"We write what we do not speak."

A client who was initially reluctant to try journaling but did it anyway and was then blown away by what the pages had to say back to her shared the above insight with me. Her resistance reflected years of being silenced in an abusive relationship. She feared her words would be used against her. She was blocked. But then she was ready to try again, and the wisdom poured out of her in a way she could finally hear and honor. She was safe to access what had always been available to her, and this was all it took to supercharge her path to healing on every level.

My client's story, although special in its own right, is not unique. I can't count the number of times I have heard the phrase, "I have tried, but journaling doesn't work for me." Therefore, they stopped the practice without the awareness as to why it felt hard and underwhelming despite all the good things they had heard about it. If you can relate, you will soon understand the power of journaling and what you can do to maximize its impact. And if you have experienced the benefits of journaling, I hope to bring you a newfound appreciation for everything the practice provides while deepening your motivation to continue.

WHY WRITE?

Quite simply, writing creates a space for our soul to speak so we can hear it. We've most likely been raised to silence parts of ourselves in order to belong. Specifically, we came into this world designed to love our caregivers unconditionally. Unfortunately, we are met with conditions in return. In response, we amplify some ways of being and dim others in order to be safe so they will love and care for us. As creatures born completely dependent, our entire survival depends on it.

Some of us responded to our circumstances by becoming the most capable one, focused on caring for others without much regard for ourselves. Others threw themselves into achieving to receive the love and attention they craved that was dependent on achieving success. Still others learned to live by perpetually watching for the slightest sign of trouble and then silenced themselves to prevent situations from becoming even worse. People do what they need to do to survive. Humans are really good at it.

But in the process of surviving, we get disconnected from our authenticity, from the truth of who we are.

The patterns of thinking and being that emerge are adaptations; they are not our actual "personality." Life wants us to allow our true self to emerge from underneath the adaptations we've taken on to survive the unconsciousness we were born into. Indeed, coming into ourselves in this lifetime is our only purpose.

Here's what's really interesting: No matter what you experienced in your early years, you have always known what you needed to thrive and come into who you are. All you and I have ever needed is love. We need a chance to be seen and loved just for *being*. We need empathy. We need support. We need to have people in our lives who are curious about our experiences and help us make sense of them. This is how our worth becomes something we never question.

We all need this. We know it in our bones. It is built into our DNA. But in this world, this kind of experience of being truly loved and seen without conditions is, unfortunately, rare.

Here's another truth: We are all equipped to create whatever is needed in order to thrive. That's right. No matter what you've survived, you do not have to be a victim of those circumstances. **You can choose to give all the love you ever needed to yourself, and you can learn how to practice that effectively.** This is what journaling can do for you.

So as much as journaling will help you get crystal clear about yourself, this practice is essentially one of self-love. It creates the loving and empathic environment we all need to feel safe to express ourselves so we can connect with our inner wisdom and discover who we are in the process. It is a practice of re-parenting ourselves in the way we always needed, so we can give ourselves the chance to emerge fully and grow into the magnificence of who we are.

One of the immediate benefits of journaling on a regular basis is a profound sense of clarity. It's interesting—for me and many others, the voice that appears on the page tends to meander in the beginning, but it eventually gets really direct. The message that emerges is simple, clear. It almost feels as if another voice comes through me, and yet it is written with my own hands. Maybe it is the wise mind, the higher self I am accessing. Perhaps it's a higher consciousness, a guide that whispers to me and whose voice I amplify in the practice. Maybe it's all of this; I don't know for sure. But it's incredibly impactful. In fact, it changed my life.

I have always had a relationship with writing. As a child, I wrote lots of stories and plays, revealing to my teachers all sorts of situations my family and I were experiencing (much to my mom's chagrin). Yes, my innocent self was a bit of an open book. The page was my medium. But my formal education killed that for me. I pursued the sciences, and there was little room left in my day-to-day to express my creativity. My path expanded my analytical skills but didn't allow me to play.

Building my own business pushed me back into fostering my creativity and renewed my dedication to showing up more authentically than ever. I knew from the start that authenticity was the only way for me to attract the right clients. But while I knew this intellectually, the prospect of putting myself out there paralyzed me.

My initial blog posts were terrible. Bland, boring, and clinical, they focused too much on presenting myself as an expert and shared data aligned in the way I was trained: objectively and without feeling. I knew I needed to move beyond the credentials and the restrictions of being "professional" to allow people to connect with my humanity. I needed to be vulnerable. I needed to accept criticism from my peers. I needed to risk rejection, or even worse, being completely ignored. I needed to break through all the fears and hurt I had experienced over never quite feeling like I belonged, over being the outsider. If I was going to fulfill my mission and have a big impact, I had no choice but to push myself through all the pain from my past and experience whatever existed on the other side of fear.

This is where my own journey as a human dovetailed with the mission I had set for my private practice: to fundamentally change the conversation about mental health to shift from "What's wrong with you?" to "What happened to you?" and empower people with tools and the knowledge that they actually have the solution within themselves. I had witnessed this transformation with countless clients in my role as a psychologist, and it was time for others to understand it too.

So there I was, advocating for authenticity while frozen in my ability to express myself. I clearly needed to step off the pedestal and embrace the struggle. I needed to walk the talk. So that's what I did. I leaned on my training and experience as a psychologist to create a signature way of journaling that made all the difference. My Flow to Grow Journaling Method helped me reconnect with my voice, create content with ease, become an expert at accessing and honoring my inner knowing, and gain the courage and confidence to design the life of my dreams. You can do it all too.

WHAT'S THE FLOW TO GROW JOURNALING METHOD?

Before I share the method, it's worth spending a little time with the setup, because every element is important.

Kick it old school—write, don't type: The most effective way to write in order to access your truth is with a writing instrument you can hold in your hand. The pen or pencil is an extension of your body. A keyboard is not. Even if you communicate in the most intimate ways with your phone or computer, it is just not the same as writing with a pen or a pencil. Think about it. On that same device, you read and respond to emails, text to-do lists, and scroll endlessly on social media. And no matter what your intentions are on that device, there are endless distractions that make it difficult to focus. None of this is conducive to flow, and flow is what's needed to bypass the thinking brain and get to the truth in our hearts.

Comfort is key: Make it cozy. This practice of self-love should feel like a warm hug, especially when times are tough. So, bring in the pillows, the blanket, maybe a warm cup of tea, and light a candle. Do whatever feels lovely to you. Create that cozy corner.

Boundaries make it better: Boundaries drive focus, which is why we create deadlines. When it comes to expressing ourselves, not having a fixed time to journal can leave us staring into space for minutes without a word ever landing on the page. Instead, decide on a timeframe in advance that you are going to use to journal. I usually give myself fifteen minutes, but ten is good too. And if that seems too long, maybe give yourself two to three minutes. It doesn't really matter. Just set the timer, and once it starts, so do you.

Begin with the breath: There is no better way to get grounded than to focus on the breath. It encourages us to gaze inward, to pay attention to where we are in the moment, and to step into the role of the observer of our own experience. After a few deep exhales followed by even deeper inhales, we can shift our consciousness out of the busyness and into a brain wave pattern called the alpha-theta state, a magical state the brain naturally falls into just before we go to sleep and for the first twenty minutes after we wake up. It is here that our creative and intuitive brain is most active, and it's from this place that most of our best ideas come.

Amplify radical self-compassion: Honesty requires safety. And for most, we need to be given permission to say anything and know that all will be okay.

Now on to the method. **The Flow to Grow Journaling Method is a way to practice showing up with radical self-compassion, which is the most profound form of love there is. Period.**

Not sure how to do it? No worries. I created a mantra of sorts to help.

Place one hand or both over your heart or heart center (the middle of your chest). This position is the invitation to bring forward and tenderly hold the most vulnerable part of you.

Imagine speaking to your vulnerable self. If it helps, picture them. For me, she is always a young child, typically around seven or eight years old, with braids fastened with baubles on the sides of her head. I know her well, and I have already made the decision to love her. As I hold my vulnerable self and breathe deeply, I say the following three phrases to her:

"There is nothing you could possibly say, think, or feel that would ever compromise my regard for you."

"There is nothing you could possibly say, think, or feel that would ever compromise my respect for you."

"There is nothing you could possibly say, think, or feel that would ever compromise my love for you."

If this is hard for you to say to yourself, that's okay. Many of us become emotional the first time we hear ourselves echoing what we have always wanted to experience. Allow the emotions to surface. And know if this is happening, it is not a sign to stop. Quite the contrary. It is an indication that more of the same is exactly what you need. Keep going.

Flow: Pick up the pen. Start the timer and write nonstop until time's up. That's it.

The only thing to do next is to try it. I have witnessed people experience amazing growth through the journaling process and in my online, private community space where we routinely meet to write in our Flow to Grow journals and share insights. The inspiration is off the charts.

Before you go, here is a poem that flowed through me and onto the pages of my journal at a time when I was faced with my own self-doubt. It took as long for me to write it as it will for you to read it.

We are all stars
Who fell from the heavens
Shining so bright
Who at some point decided to dim the light
To get along, to fit in
We let the darkness of doubt win
Then spent a lifetime
Searching
For the light that is our birthright
So we can return home.

Shine bright, my love. Shine bright.

Chapter NINETEEN

PRACTICING GRATITUDE

To Luc, who is always there through the thick and thin, and my three daughters, who keep me in the loop of what is and isn't " in" or " hip." Also, to all the women who surround me, thank you for making sure I pursue my dreams.

LYNN HARRISON

Lynn Harrison transitioned from a successful twenty-year corporate career to becoming a catalyst for empowerment and transformation. As the founder of @lessonswithlynn, Lynn is a certified high-per-formance coach dedicated to helping women craft the lives they envision, regardless of their stage in life. With a holistic approach to personal development, Lynn is also a certified yoga instructor who focuses on mobility and functional movement, as well as a certified stretching stretching and breath-work coach. She firmly believes that true transformation originates from within and integrates mind, body, and spirit. Balancing her professional endeavors, Lynn nurtures a bustling household as a loving wife and a mother to three grown daughters and two dogs. Beyond her professional and personal commitments, Lynn is engaged in community service as the therapy dog coordinator for St. John Ambulance.

www.lessonswithlynn.com
@lessonswithlynn

GRATITUDE IS A
STRENGTH THAT
PROVIDES YOU CLARITY
ON WHAT IS IMPORTANT
TO YOU AND KEEPS YOU
ALIGNED WITH YOUR
VALUES.

Growing up, I watched my dad work hard and strive for success, always aiming for more. Perhaps that's why, back then, I saw gratitude as a way for people to simply settle for what they had, avoiding the need to aim higher. I thought being content meant you weren't willing to work hard or take risks to improve your situation. I would say I even pushed it to the point of thinking it was a character flaw. If people thought they were happy with what they had, it meant they didn't need to work hard or risk anything to get more. That was not me. I've wanted more for as long as I can remember.

When I met Luc, my husband of thirty-plus years, we were in our third year of university. It didn't take me long to figure out that Luc was one of *those* people. He was thankful for everything, even the simplest things in life. He would point to things when we went for walks, saying how beautiful they were, or he'd be curious about how a tree looked. He'd always stare in wonder at what we'd see. Out of all the wonderful aspects of Luc I fell in love with, this particular way of being was not one of them. It annoyed me!

Luc and I had good jobs, got married, lived in a brand-new condo, traveled, and enjoyed a few years of marital bliss. Eventually, we expanded our family to include one, then two daughters—healthy, beautiful, talented individual little personalities that melted my heart. Luc was overjoyed and so content, and so was I . . . until I wasn't. I felt there was, and should be, more. We *should* get better jobs to make more money. We *should* find a bigger house to have more room for the girls. Many of our friends and family members seemed to have more than we did. I could always find the ones who had bigger houses, nicer clothes, better careers, more exciting lives . . . more, more, more. And Luc would tell me, "Look what we have. Look how fortunate we are." It got my blood boiling. I could not understand why he didn't want more than what we had, and I began thinking his contentment meant he lacked motivation.

For years, when I would get to my lowest point of desperation, he would respond with something along the lines of "I'm grateful for what we do have. I don't envy what others have. Why does what someone else have affect how you feel about yourself or what we have?" Those words used to send me into a spiral. He just could not understand why I refused to be content and happy about what we did have. He would then refer to other parts of the world and to less-privileged people and tell me to compare myself to those who didn't have as much as we did. I'd say, "Why can't you look up to the ones who have more and want to reach for that?" It was a debate that went on for many years; it was always in the middle of our arguments. We agreed to disagree, except he continued pointing out things in subtle ways.

One year, Luc heard Robin Sharma speak, then encouraged me to read his book *The Monk Who Sold His Ferrari*. I did, and my attitude toward gratitude began to shift. Reading the proverb "I cursed the day I had no shoes until I saw the man who had no feet" was enlightening. What I quickly realized was that I could learn and practice gratitude. To this day, I truly believe it has been one of my most challenging things to do. But once I did commit and really understood how it worked, it became like a scavenger hunt. I would go through my day, looking out for people, experiences, or things to be grateful for experiencing.

I remember a specific time in my life a few years ago when I fully embraced gratitude at a whole new level. I began recognizing that sometimes, more often than I ever imagined, we become grateful for the challenges and difficulties life throws at us. Those tough moments can be exactly what we need, and the challenge we must overcome shows us what we're made of. Those are moments I never want to take for granted again. They are often the moments that define who we are and who we will become.

Journaling has also made a huge difference. When I write down things I am grateful for, it sticks, I embody it, and I can expand on it to capture it. And the best part is, I can reread how I felt at certain times during my life, just like I did when writing this chapter. When you write down what you are grateful for, the feeling has more permanence, and you have a written record of it.

If you journal about only one thing, make it gratitude.

When I began practicing gratitude, I found it less difficult to be thankful when everything was seemingly going well. Finding things to be grateful for seems so much easier when you are feeling happy, free, and lucky to have it all. And once you identify one thing, then something else comes to light, then another. Miraculously, you no longer need to look for things to be grateful for, they come naturally to you. During these times, being grateful seems easy.

It also seems more accessible in times of despair. If you are about to lose something or someone important to you, you become immensely grateful to have them in your life. When the universe threatens to take something away from us, gratitude comes to us far more easily than in the middle of a mundane day when gratefulness may be more difficult to practice.

I certainly experienced this when Luc and I almost lost our eldest daughter to a skiing accident. She fell and was lying unconscious face down in the snow about two hundred meters from her skis, with blood dripping out of her helmet and mask. She remained unconscious for several minutes and then drifted in and out for hours while at the hospital where we, as non-patients, were not allowed in due to a COVID outbreak. While she was unconscious, I had no trouble practicing gratitude. I was simply so grateful we'd found her, so grateful the safety patrols had come fairly quickly, so grateful the ambulance had arrived immediately and had gotten her to the nearest hospital. It allowed me to feel calm even though I was terrified about the possible outcome.

The first twenty-four hours after her accident were turbulent. We had some scary calls from the hospital staff, and the following day, they asked us to come in despite the outbreak. We knew it couldn't be good. On the forty-five-minute ride to the hospital that afternoon, all we did was recall all the wonderful moments we'd had as a family, the wonderful life Emilie had had in her short twenty-four years. We told ourselves that no matter what happened, she'd had a great life. It might seem a little morbid or cold reading these words, and I might have felt that way too if I had not been practicing gratitude all these years, but this memory is recorded in my journal, so I know it's how we were feeling at the time.

When you are faced with these kinds of situations, when you come close to losing someone, you become so thankful for so much else. You want to make sure you don't continue losing things, so you take stock of everything for which you are truly thankful. Our gratitude practice helped us throughout our daughter's journey to recovery, especially in the most challenging and emotionally driven moments, because we were just so thankful she was alive and going to make a full recovery.

Another example of gratefulness in my life occurred at the airport a few years ago when I made a really bad decision to crawl under the safety barrier at the lineup to Customs. My backpack caught the strap, and as I turned my head to see what had happened, the strap—the hard plastic end of it—snapped free and hit me straight in the middle of my left eye. The impact was like nothing I had ever experienced. I immediately felt a black curtain come down inside my eye. The pulsing and shooting pain were incredible, but what scared me the most was the blackness blocking my vision. I couldn't see anything through the eye. I was scared and anxious for about two seconds, then my mind immediately went to all the things I'd been fortunate to see over the years. I began listing all the faces, places, and colors. It was an incredible feeling, and I assure you I would have reacted much differently several years before I started to intentionally practice gratitude.

I remember thinking at the time: *If I had known this was the last time I would see clearly in my life, I would have paid more attention to EVERY-THING!* This memory has stuck with me. To this day I have "floaters" in both my eyes and have blurry vision 85 percent of the time, which is very distracting and can be annoying. But I have never complained because I am so grateful for all the years my vision was clear, crisp, and sharp. I am also very grateful for what I can see, and I will continue to live my life every day, even if it is a little more dim, with the knowledge that it could be so much worse. I take time to appreciate the little things I can see, hear, taste, and feel, as I know they can be taken away so quickly.

There are many gratitude practices in the world, but the best one for you *to* do is the one you *will* do.

HERE'S HOW YOU CAN PRACTICE GRATITUDE:

Start and end your days with THANK YOU. For every day, event, challenge, and experience, try to remember to say thank you for all of them.

Each night, think about what you liked about the day. Try to capture something good, regardless of how the day evolved. There is always at least one thing to be grateful for in each day, even if it means you simply got through it.

Treat it like a treasure hunt. Each day, search for life's delights. You'll look for one, then suddenly another one appears. They seem to pop up once you're open to discovering them, receiving them, and recognizing them. You can focus your energy on everything that is wrong in your life, OR you can focus on what's right. It's your choice.

Reflect on the simple things. Think of those things that if absent, you would miss and do anything to have them back. That is a form of gratitude.

You'll notice that as you become better at practicing gratitude, the things you are thankful for may no longer be of monetary value or tangible presence: your health and the health of your family members, your ability to see, hear, hug, smile, breathe, etc.

I worked on my yoga certification a few years ago, and more recently, my breath-coach certification. You may wonder how something as simple as breathing needs practice. Let me tell you, most of us need the practice, and I feel it is the same with gratitude. How we manage, control, and balance our nervous system is pivotal in that it allows us to focus on gratitude. For me, instead of being in a state of fight or flight or wired and tired, which usually has me focusing on scarcity and the need for more, I find myself in a state of openness, a state that allows me to respond calmly to external stimuli and have space to reflect on gratitude more easily. Through practice, I have elevated my gratitude to another level, just as I have my breathing techniques. Once you begin practicing, you become more aware of how to be grateful.

The more you practice the awareness of gratitude, the more your mind approaches each day on the lookout for things to be grateful about.

With practice, you will notice you go throughout your day searching for what you are grateful for instead of what you want or need. What's even more fascinating is that it truly reduces feelings of envy that sometimes creep up when you compare yourself to others. When gratitude is your focus, you'll be amazed by the richness of your life.

Gratitude is not the enemy of motivation and drive. Gratitude is a strength that provides you clarity on what is important to you and keeps you aligned with your values. Thus, I encourage you to be grateful for what you do have rather than wasting time and energy on what you don't. You'll soon see how easy it becomes to be grateful and begin truly loving the life you're leading.

Chapter TWENTY

FINDING YOUR COMMUNITY

To the many incredible women I have had the privilege
of serving over the last few years, I do this work for you!

LIANNE KIM

Lianne Kim is a business coach, the founder and CEO of the Mamas & Co. community, and the host of the popular podcast *The Business of Thinking Big*. Her two decades of sales and marketing experience help people create successful, profitable, joyful businesses so they can live their wildest dreams. She lives in Toronto with her husband and two children.

www.liannekim.com
@liannekimcoach

FEELING A SENSE OF BELONGING IS ACTUALLY CRUCIAL TO OVERALL MENTAL HEALTH, WHICH MEANS IT IS CRUCIAL TO OUR ABILITY TO ENJOY OUR LIFE.

@liannekimcoach

The memory is still burned into my brain. I am a young girl, about five or six years old. I can hear them on the other side of the door, my brother and sister who are four and six years older than I am, respectively. They are snickering, trying to hold in their laughter, but failing miserably. They are laughing at me.

I can feel the hot tears streaming down my red cheeks as I bang on the door and scream at them to stop. My heart is pounding inside my small but enraged body. I am crying so hard I am sweating. I am in so much emotional pain that I feel it physically, like I am actually going to burst.

"Stop it!" I yell. "Stop laughing at me!" I am desperate to be heard. To be taken seriously for once. I am so angry that I want to hurt some-body, but I know that I can't, so instead, I pound even harder on my bedroom door. This awful blend of anger, shame, and loneliness is unlike any other pain I know.

They continue to laugh as they muster an apology, something they are instructed to do by my mother. Her compassionate soul can see that their teasing has wounded me, and so when I storm off back to my room to get away from my tormentors, she tells them they have to apologize to me to make the situation right. Unfortunately, it only makes the situation worse, and now I feel even more horrible than before.

Being the youngest sucks! To not be listened to, to not be included, to not be taken seriously is the absolute worst feeling in the world. *They never want to play with me; they don't ever include me. They're just mean to me. They make fun of me and leave me out of everything. It's not right!*

Now I can hear my mother on the other side of the door. "You have to stop laughing. Just say you're sorry and go." They finally comply. Their laughs turn to giggles, then a few quiet murmurs as they leave.

As I hear them walk away, my rage slowly dissipates. My heart rate slows. My breath normalizes. My face still feels hot and sticky from tears, so I wipe them away. I feel calmer. I am no longer so angry, but I do have one very strong feeling that lingers . . .

I feel alone.

I am sure I am not the only person on the planet to have had an experience like this one. All humans go through feelings of isolation at some point. For some, me included, this repeats throughout their life. As my siblings matured and I got older, their teasing subsided, but the cracks in my confidence were already established.

Similar isolating episodes at school and later at work gnawed at me:

Being banished from my middle school friend group because I didn't dress a certain way.

Not fitting in at a workplace that was particularly cliquey and eventually getting a demotion.

Getting publicly shamed on social media and having many so-called friends pile on.

And with each fresh experience of feeling like I didn't belong, there were the same old stories on a loop in my mind:

I don't fit in.

I am not good enough.

Nobody likes me.

I am a loser.

These demeaning stories are what we all tell ourselves at one point or another, often on the heels of an experience that leaves us feeling like we're on the outside looking in. And these stories don't only play during big moments; often it's the small, seemingly insignificant moments that spur the inner negative dialogue. Perhaps you can relate:

Your friend thanks everyone for the group gift, except for you.

You "accidentally" get left off the invite list for the neighborhood block party.

Your colleagues all get mentioned in the company newsletter, but you don't.

There is a gift for everyone in the family under the Christmas tree, except for you (this one actually happened to me!).

It would take me decades to realize the pain I had from a feeling of lack of belonging would actually lead to my life's mission.

Human beings have a deep need for a sense of belonging. It's innate. Feeling excluded, ignored, or alone can eat away at our confidence and our mental health. For years, psychologists have argued that feeling a part of a group, part of a community, is vital.

In fact, in his 1943 groundbreaking work, Maslow's Hierarchy of Needs, influential psychologist Abraham Maslow classified "belonging and love" as one of the main necessities for life after the basic needs of food, water, and shelter. And as he stated, this social aspect is not something we can find within ourselves: "The needs for safety, belonging, love relations and for respect can be satisfied only by other people, i.e., only from outside the person." The truth is that we need others—we need a community.

This is something that author Dan Buettner uncovered firsthand while studying Blue Zones. During his extensive research around the world, he found that the human beings who live the longest all share similar attributes, regardless of geography or ethnicity. And one of those commonalities is that they all have strong familial and social networks, thus proving that community is a key element in longevity.

Having a community helps us feel better by creating a sense of psychological safety. When we feel alone, we might feel weak or vulnerable. But when we belong to someone or something, we feel secure in knowing that we will be taken care of, that we're protected.

Therefore, feeling a sense of belonging is actually crucial to overall mental health, which means it is crucial to our ability to enjoy our life.

WHAT IS COMMUNITY?

Community, as I see it, is any group of people with whom you share common values, beliefs, and struggles. When you have a community around you, that means you have people who know you, who care about you, and who feel you are one of them. When you belong to a community, be it an online group or a "real life" one such as your neighborhood, you don't feel alone. You feel supported, like there's always someone who has your back.

The family you are born into is one community, although it is not one you get to choose. The neighborhood you live in is another example, as is your friend group, the people who you choose to spend time with socially. You also have a community at your place of work. You may belong to a sports team, social group, or fitness facility that provides that sense of community. Your church or place of worship can also provide a meaningful sense of belonging.

The truth is, there are a lot of different ways we can experience the concept of community, but it can also be easy to deprive ourselves from others. Often, socializing seems like a chore or another thing on our daily to-do lists. I know a lot of working mothers who are so busy working a full-time job or running a business and raising a family that they neglect to spend time with anyone else. They tell themselves they don't have time for friends or a social life, and soon enough, it starts to impact their mental health.

I will also say that one of the most isolated groups I've ever encountered is mom entrepreneurs. These warriors juggle raising a family with growing a business, most of them alone, often from home, day in and day out. They spend hours on end working by themselves and not talking to any other adults. Not only that, but they also don't have work peers who they can commiserate with or a superior who can provide feedback. Every decision they make, every move they take, is all on them. And that can be a scary and lonely feeling.

It is for this reason that I founded my community back in 2014. I was about to start working more seriously on my business, while working from home in my day job. I had two kids under the age of three, and I was terrified of spending all day at home, alone, with virtually no contact with the outside world.

So, I started an online group for mamapreneurs and began hosting in-person meetups every month for the sole purpose of having one evening a month on the calendar that I would look forward to, one night when I could be in community with my fellow mom bosses where we could talk about business, family, and life.

I needed those nights because my mom friends didn't run businesses, and the people I did know who ran businesses were not moms. When I spent time with my fellow "mom bosses," I really felt like I could be myself. I knew that whatever I shared with them, they could relate to my struggles and possibly offer some advice or encouragement. And I desperately needed that.

As a result, the one place I felt the most myself was the place I created!

And that online group I started back in 2014 is about to celebrate its ten-year anniversary (at the time of writing). The reason this group has stood the test of time is because I built something that women desperately need—a place where they feel they belong.

HOW TO FIND YOUR COMMUNITY:

There are two ways you can find community: You can join an existing community, or you can create your own. I chose the latter because there just weren't a lot of groups for mamapreneurs at the time.

Here are some things to consider when looking to join or create your own community:

What do I feel is missing in my life? It's important to think about what you'd like in a group. For example, maybe you're looking to get more physically fit but that's not a desire of your current circle. Or perhaps you're craving more spirituality in your life.

What do I value most? Finding groups of people who share common values and beliefs you wish to nurture in yourself is a good place to start. It's important that you surround yourself with people who share similar core values as it will create that sense of belonging.

What kind of energy will help me thrive? If you're looking to grow a business, you need positive, motivated people around you. If you're looking to create more calm in your life, you might want people who are more Zen in nature.

How much time do I have to devote to my new community? Some groups or clubs can be very time-consuming, while others are less demanding. Knowing how much you have to give can be a helpful deciding factor.

Where do I want to meet? Do you want an in-person community or an online one? When I first started my community in 2014, meeting in person was a big need for me. As my business grew and I had less time, it became more important to meet online.

Who do I know that might also want or need these things? One of the reasons why my community was successful was because I had met a handful of women who also craved support with their businesses, so I started there. I didn't wait until I had dozens of people; I hosted our first meeting with just seven women.

The point is, you can start where you are and build the community you need. Ask your friends or post on social media that you're looking to start or join a group. Share the things you are looking for in a community and ask for recommendations of existing groups, or you can ask to be connected to other people with similar interests.

It may not seem like it right now, but you likely know at least a few people who are also craving connection and support who share similar interests and values as you do, but you won't know until you put it out there. The universe has a funny way of delivering exactly what we need, once we declare that we need it.

Like everything in life, the longer you put off just starting, the longer you put off getting to reap the benefits. And the benefits are plenty! By connecting with others, you'll feel fulfilled, calm, and secure with a sense of higher purpose by sharing with and contributing to others. The right community can absolutely lead to you living as your healthiest, happiest self, so go find yours!

Mamas & Co.

WORKS CITED

CHAPTER 3: RECHARGE & THRIVE: THE TRANSFORMATIONAL POWER OF SLEEP

Huffington, Arianna. 2017. *The Sleep Revolution: Transforming Your Life, One Night at a Time*. Harmony; Reprint edition.

Walker, Matthew. 2017. *Why We Sleep: Unlocking the Power of Sleep and Dreams*. Scribner; Reprint edition.

CHAPTER 4: THE FAR-REACHING BENEFITS OF FLEXIBILITY

Howard E. LeWine, MD, reviewer, "The importance of stretching," *Harvard Health Publishing*, April 17, 2024, https://www.health.harvard.edu/staying-healthy/the-importance-of-stretching.

CHAPTER 7: STAND UP FOR YOUR HEALTH

Robert N. Butler, MD, "Public Interest Report No. 23: Exercise, the Neglected Therapy," *The International Journal of Aging and Human Development*, Vol. 8(2), 1977-78, https://journals.sagepub.com/doi/abs/10.2190/AM1W-RABB-4PJY-P1PK?journalCode=ahdb.

Ratey, John J., MD. 2013. *Spark: The Revolutionary New Science of Exercise and the Brain*. Little, Brown Spark; Reprint edition.

Langer, Ellen. 2007. "Mind-Set Matters: Exercise and the Placebo Effect." *Psychological Science*. 18. 165-71. 10.1111/j.1467-9280.2007.01867.x.

Gottfried, Sara, MD. 2018. *Younger: A Breakthrough Program to Reset Your Genes, Reverse Aging, and Turn Back the Clock 10 Years*. HarperOne; Reprint edition.

O'Mara, Shane. 2020. *In Praise of Walking: The New Science of How We Walk and Why It's Good for Us*. Vintage.

CHAPTER 9: CREATING CLARETY BY PLUNGING INTO THE COLD

Weitzel, Kristin. Personal communication with author. June 16, 2024.

CHAPTER 10: THE HEALING TABLE

Rosalind Chia-Yu Chen, Meei-Shyuan Lee, Yu-Hung Chang, and Mark L. Wahlqvist. "Cooking frequency may enhance survival in Taiwanese elderly." *Cambridge University Press*. May 11, 2011.

O. M. Thompson, C. Ballew, K. Resnicow, A. Must, L. G. Bandini, H. Cyr, W. H. Dietz. "Food purchased away from home as a predictor of change in BMI z-score among girls." *PubMed*. February 28, 2004.

CHAPTER 11: HOW YOUR BODY LANGUAGE CAN BOOST YOUR CONFIDENCE

Kleck, Robert & Strenta, Angelo. 1980. "Perceptions of the impact of negatively valued characteristics on social interaction." *Journal of Personality and Social Psychology.* 39. 861-873. 10.1037/0022-3514.39.5.861.

Carney, Dana R.; Cuddy, Amy J.C.; Yap, Andy J. January 10, 2010. "Power Posing: Brief Nonverbal Displays Affect Neuroendocrine Levels and Risk Tolerance." *Psychological Science.* 21 (10): 1363–1368.

CHAPTER 13: GET OUTSIDE!

O'Mara, Shane. 2020. *In Praise of Walking: The New Science of How We Walk and Why It's Good for Us.* Vintage.

Lisa Marshall, Melinda Ratini, MS, DO (reviewer), "Get Morning Light, Sleep Better at Night," *WebMD*, March 23, 2022, https://www.webmd.com/sleep-disorders/features/morning-light-better-sleep

Jessica Stanhope, Martin F. Breed, Philip Weinstein. "Exposure to greenspaces could reduce the high global burden of pain." *PubMed.* August 2020.

CHAPTER 16: PLANTS FOR A BETTER LIFE

Nasa Technology Transfer Program, "NASA Plant Research Offers a Breath of Fresh Air" https://spinoff.nasa.gov/Spinoff2019/cg_7.html

CHAPTER 17: WHAT'S BEST FOR YOU?

"Unseen Yet Too Visible," Peanut, accessed September 10, 2024, https://invisible-mothers.peanut-app.io/.

Lisa Bilyeu, host, *Women of Impact*, podcast, "Take Your Power Back In 2024 - Master Confidence, Set Boundaries & Create A New You | Jameela Jamil," January 10, 2024, https://podcasts.apple.com/tz/podcast/take-your-power-back-in-2024-master-confidence-set/id1435217865?i=1000641190342

Manson, Mark. 2016. *The Subtle Art of Not Giving a F*ck: A Counterintuitive Approach to Living a Good Life.* Harper; 2nd edition.

Brown, Brené. 2021. *Atlas of the Heart: Mapping Meaningful Connection and the Language of Human Experience.* Random House.

Louise Hay, Facebook, February 22, 2013, https://www.facebook.com/louiselhay/posts/i-let-go-of-all-expectations-people-places-and-things-are-free-to-be-themselves-/10151534000914750/?locale=ms_MY.

CHAPTER 19: PRACTICING GRATITUDE

Sharma, Robin. 1999. *The Monk Who Sold His Ferrari: A Fable About Fulfilling Your Dreams & Reaching Your Destiny.* HarperSanFrancisco.

CHAPTER 20: FINDING YOUR COMMUNITY

Abraham Maslow, 1943, "A theory of human motivation," *Psychological Review.* 50 (4): 370–396.

fEMPOWER Publications Inc. is a boutique publishing house and community serving purpose-driven women in the pursuit of big dreams. We offer full-service book production and publication, thought-leadership development programs, and collaborative writing opportunities for females of all ages.

www.fempower.pub

 @fempower.pub
 @fempower.pub

Join the Author{ity} Membership